The 'Real' Ramakrishna

As I Have Come to Know Him
As Ramakrishna's Child

(From the pen of a totally non-traditional Ramakrishna scholar)

Books Published by Allied Publishers for Dr. Siddhartha Ganguli

1. Live Happily, Work Happily - 2009
2. SUCCESS Can be Planned and Earned - 2010
3. Greying Gracefully: Planning for Retirement and Old Age Happiness - 2011
4. Conscious Management - 2011
5. The Making of a Winning Child - 2012
6. Smart Leading and Parenting of Teenage Kids in the Digital Era - 2021
7. Music is Magic Music is Medicine: Impact of Music on Body, Brain, Mind & Soul - 2023
8. The Four Moons in the Human Body - The Mysterious Tales of the Bauls of Bengal (Introducing 'BaulOlogy') - 2023
9. Love: A Good MedicineThe Saga of the Elixir of Life (Introducing 'LoveOlogy') - 2024
10. Goddess Kali God Thoughts Sri Sri Ramakrishna A Few Slices of Sri Sri Ramakrishna's Soul (Introducing 'SoulOlogy') - 2024

The 'Real' Ramakrishna

As I Have Come to Know Him
As Ramakrishna's Child

(From the pen of a totally non-traditional Ramakrishna scholar)

Siddhartha Ganguli, ***PhD***

ALLIED PUBLISHERS PVT. LTD.

Noida • Mumbai • Kolkata • Chennai • Bangalore

ALLIED PUBLISHERS PRIVATE LIMITED

D-5, Sector-2, **Noida**–201 301
Ph. Nos.: 0120-4320295/2542557/4352866
E-mail: delhi.books@alliedpublishers.com

17 Chittaranjan Avenue, **Kolkata**–700072
Ph.: 033-22129618 • E-mail: cal.books@alliedpublishers.com

15 J.N. Heredia Marg, Ballard Estate, **Mumbai**–400001
Ph.: 022-42126969 • E-mail: mumbai.books@alliedpublishers.com

No. 25/10, Commander-in-Chief Road, Ethiraj Lane (Next to Post Office)
Egmore, **Chennai**–600008
Ph.: 044-28223938 • E-mail: chennai.books@alliedpublishers.com

P.B. No. 9932, No. 15, 3rd Floor (Next to Vijaya Bank), 5th Cross, Gandhinagar,
Karnataka, **Bangalore**–560009. Ph.: 080-41530285/22386239
E-mail: bngl.books@alliedpublishers.com

Website: www.alliedpublishers.com

ISBN: 978-93-89934-33-5

The concept for the front cover design has been contributed by the author's young creative friend Andy J. Peters of Manchester, England, UK.

Published by Sunil Sachdev and printed by Ravi Sachdev
at Allied Publishers Pvt. Ltd., D-5, Sector-2, Noida–201 301

Dedication

To the immortal soul of
Avatar Sri Sri Ramakrishna

Gratitude

This is my second English book project on Sri Sri Ramakrishna. I was first motivated to get engaged in deep research on Sri Sri Ramakrishna by Tapan Kumar Ghosh of Sahityasree of Kolkata who are one of my Bengali publishers. That motivation has now turned into a *drive* to continue my looking at the *Avatar* from angles which no Ramakrishna scholar has done so far. My first gratitude is to him and also to the North Bengal novelist Amal Krishna Roy who introduced me to Mr Ghosh.

I am deeply indebted to my dear wife Utpala and our three children, Abhishek Abhirup and Ishita who have taken unceasing interest in all my desk research and book writing & publishing projects. As usual, my Personal Secretary Pervez Alam was always available to help me out whenever I needed his assistance. I share with him a slice of the blessings that Avatar Ramakrishna has been showering on me. Without the Avatar's blessings, it would not have been possible for me to continue my scholarly pursuits on the Godman in right earnest.

I would like to thank Allied Publishers Pvt. Ltd., the leading Indian publishing house with international connections for undertaking the responsibility of executing this book project and also for marketing & promoting the volume worldwide. I fail to find the right expressions to thank Jagdish Singh of Allied's Editorial Dept. and his colleagues who have handled the project with total dedication evident from the fast speed of their editorial services extended to me.

I'm indebted to the Ramakrishna scholars in India and abroad whose works have enriched my knowledge about the Indian saint.

Contents

Who is Ramakrishna?

Sri Sri Ramakrishna to Goddess Kali

"Neither do I wish to be immortal
Nor do I have any tall claim!

The only purpose for which I'm born
Is to get you!

I've been born many times earlier
And have also died on your lap!

But I've not been liberated from mortality
As I wanted to see and be with you
again and again!!

(Adapted from an award-winning Bengali song by the famous Bengali songwriter and singer Kabir Suman but composed differently in English for the present volume)

"It is an almost impossible task to know, to understand the REAL Ramakrishna. The Paramhansa was gracious enough to expose his REAL Self to some who deserved."

"Ramakrishna's father knew that he was an *avatar*, Lord Raghubir in new form. Monk Totapuri also came to know him. So did the Bhairavi Brahmani. Ramakrishna's sister (Hriday's mother) also recognised his super-naturality; that is why she worshipped him."

"Some of his contemporaries also came to know him as an *avatar*; that is due to his own grace."

"His own nephew Hriday, his constant companion, could not recognise him. He knew him as his uncle."

"Even if you stay near, you cannot get to know the REAL in people. You can know only when he exposes his REAL Self".

Adapted from Sri M, author of *Sri Ramkrishna Kathamrita* [1]

Akshay Kumar Sen, the creator of *Ramakrishna Punthi* has described Sri Sri Ramakrishna as **Hidden *Avatar*** (In Bengali: 'Gupta *Avatar*'). In this context, he has elaborated in his book *Sri Sri Ramakrishna Mahima*:

> "It is indeed too difficult to know Ramakrishna Dev. There are no *rajasic* glare (glamour and display) in him. From the beginning till the end, he is an embodiment of *sattvic* wealth (purity and renunciation). It is most difficult for an ordinary devotee to recognise and capture the wealth of *sattva*.
>
> There is no hair-raising fight with the demons and merciless slaying of the *asuras*. All such things are much easier for common people to understand and appreciate by witnessing and hearing from others. But here, the wealth of *sattva* – cannot be seen or heard from others' description. You need altogether different types of eyes, ears and mind.
>
> Do you know what had happened? Once, all the gems preserved in God's locker were stolen. Ramakrishna Dev used his own body and mind to recover all those gems and he had those distributed far and wide.
>
> Whatever Sri Sri Ramakrishna has made me see and hear – from those I've understood very clearly that he is God, an *avatar* of God, and the owner of the whole universe of ours. I've understood very clearly that he is the all-powerful Lord Shiva, the flute-playing Lord Krishna and the fierce-looking Goddess Kali. I've understood very clearly that he is the unabridged Satchidananda – beyond mind and intelligence on the one hand, and most comprehensible by mind and intelligence on the other. For you and me, the best way to KNOW him is to witness his sport (*leela*)."

—**Akshay Kumar Sen,**
Sri Sri Ramakrishna-Mahima, Kolkata: Udbodhan Karjalay, 2019, p. 13

"Thakur Ramakrishna had said to me that he is the Lord Jagannath of Puri himself. That is why he had sent me to Puri a number of times. Again, he had told me that he himself is Jesus Christ and also Sri Sri Chaitanya Mahaprabhu. He had told Naren that the devotees of Gour do not know that I'm Gouranga. He had said several times that he and Chaitanya are the same. He never went to Puri as he was afraid that if he were in Puri, he will lose his gross body because he will be overwhelmed by the *Mahabhava* that was characteristic of Sri Chaitanya Mahaprabhu. He knew that the old memories of his Chaitanya birth will haunt him. His gross body will not be able to withstand that force. He had also not visited Gaya for the same reason as he had anticipated that he will lose his gross body there. His anticipation was based on the fact that his *Soul* had come from Gaya."

"Thakur himself had said that he was an *avatar*. He had said that he was eternally *blissful (Satchidananda)* in his *subtle body*; however, he had got into his *gross body* to descend on earth. He had not only said that but also had shown his REAL form *(Swarupa)* to his devotees through his various *sports (leela)*. The devotees used to get amazed and used to wonder: how is it all possible for an ordinary temple priest! He was no less than a *Super Greal Soul (Paramatma)*!!"

—Translated & adapted from the Bengali book
Sriramkrishner Srimo;
by Dilip Kumar Ghosh; Kolkata: Sahityasree, 2022, p. 28.

"One who was Ram, and one who was Krishna, they are in present times, Ramakrishna!

One who was Christ and one who was Gouranga, they are in present times, manifested in me – Ramakrishna!!"

—Translated & adapted from the Bengali book
Sriramkrishner Srimo;
by Dilip Kumar Ghosh: Kolkata: Sahityasree, 2022, p. 29.

Reference

[1] *Dilip Ghosh, Sri Sri Ramakrishna Punthi: Ek Akshay Srishti* (In Bengali), Kolkata: Sahityasree, 2023, p. 158.

My Thoughts on the Father's Day

Today is the Father's Day! The day when we express gratitude from the core of our hearts to one of our twin parents. I've been toying with a different concept altogether regarding 'parentage'. We've our biological parents whose genes we share in our living tissues – the 'body' and the 'brain'. Our height, physical constitution, colour of skin, hair and the eyes as well as our brain structure we inherit from our biological parents. As regards brain, latest research has revealed that most of our forebrain structures are inherited from our mother whereas the mid-brain's limbic system (the 'emotional mind') is our father's gift to us. 'Mind' consists of inter-neuronal networks which are related to the exposure we have in life with the help of our senses including the mind which some schools regard as equivalent to a sensory organ. The 'soul' comes from outside and, according to the Hindu school of Tantra¸ a soul wandering in the space above looking for a suitable womb where it can most comfortably and conveniently pursue the unfulfilled mission of its past lives, enters at the end of the 7th week (that in 49 days) after the conception into the *Pineal Gland (PG)* of the foetus and endeavours to settle down until it is taken out of the womb to see the light of day. This 'soul' may contain a slice of your REAL father or mother who happens to be your spiritual guardian and would go on showering on you the spiritual values that would help you to develop as a complete person. Your biological parents would support you economically, provide you with all necessities for living and growing up for economic independence but they may not have the wherewithal to groom you spiritually. In some cases, they may be ruining your life totally.

I'll share a live example with you. My father Monoj Ganguli, LLB (London), Bar-at-Law (Lincoln's Inn, London) was a leading barrister at the Calcutta High Court. The Ballygunge Police Station area, where our house was located in South Calcutta was known as 'Barrister Para'. There were at least 10 barristers and judges (barristers who had become high court judges on leaving their practice) living in our locality.

Our next-door neighbour was a top barrister of Calcutta and Delhi High Courts and the Supreme Court of India. He was a brilliant man who was highly knowledgeable regarding law having obtained a PhD in Law from Cambridge University, England. But, he had a vice. He was addicted to alcohol. He would break his fast with whiskey and go on gulping until he left for the High Court. Again, on his return, he will start on his booze and continue until midnight.

This barrister uncle had two daughters, both as brilliant as he was. The elder one was studying Botany and the younger one History. The elder daughter was a Papa's girl and whenever there were no clients in his dad's chamber, she will study there with her books and copy books. She tasted whiskey and became a guzzler of alcoholic beverages – whiskey, beer, rum, gin, and vodka. There were crates full of such alcoholic beverages in Uncle's cellar and she had ready access to those. So, what I want to emphasize here is that although my barrister uncle was the girl's biological father, uncle was not her REAL father – could not instil sound spiritual values in her. Most interestingly, the family was most religious. They used to celebrate Shyma Puja in their house with big fanfare. Unfortunately, religion and spirituality are not the same – sometimes they reside at opposite poles.

There used be cocktail and dinner parties frequently at our home and the invitees were all top barristers and high court judges. Sometimes, Supreme Court judges also used to attend. And, even otherwise, in evening times, some barristers dropped in for consultation, they were offered hard drinks and not tea, coffee or soft drinks. I was like an island in the hard drinks culture. I was never attracted towards any hard or soft drinks even while studying and lecturing abroad. In my working life also, I avoided corporate cocktails and dinner parties where hard drinks were served. I was also not fond of red meat or chicken much.

While in foreign countries, my non-veg diet was limited to fried eggs and baked beans, fish fillets and finger chips, or a stuffed omelette.

Now, on Father's Day, today, I've discovered my Real Father. I strongly feel, which I've never felt earlier, that when the wandering soul entered the Pineal Gland of the foetus inside my mother Asha Ganguli's womb, forty-nine days/seven weeks after her conception, it had a slice of Sri Sri Ramakrishna's soul which has been like my armour all my life keeping me away from the most debilitating 4Ms of tantra—madya (wine), mamso (red meat), maithuna (recreational intercourse), and mudra (coins); in short, *kam* (desire) and *kanchan* (greed for wealth & prosperity, more than what you require for healthy living). I got so many offers from beautiful girls abroad, so many offers for highly-paid jobs abroad, but the slice of Sri Sri Ramakrishna's Soul in me has prevented me from getting allured. And, I've no regrets at all. I am certainly indebted to my biological parents and my biological ancestors for what all supports I've got from them, but my Real Indebtedness is to Sri Sri Ramakrishna and his mother Goddess Kali and Ma Sarada Devi for being my Real Parents. I consider myself more fortunate than Narendranath and the *Avatar*'s other disciples who lived with him and had to leave their respective families to take sannyas. I didn't have to follow their footsteps and become a R K Mission monk to pay back what I've got from Sri Ramakrishna. I've lived a very happy householder's life with my most understanding wife Utpala, now in our eighties still enjoying as best of health as possible at this advanced age.

I'm repaying all my debts to him not by offering any sweets or savouries to him or doing his puja. My service to him is to try and represent the REAL RAMAKRISHNA to the world. Who can be a better representer of the REAL RAMAKRISHNA than me in whose *Pineal Gland* he had inserted a slice of his luminous soul to be with the child all through his life until his end on this planet.

I am Ramakrishna's Child!!

Emotion for food, emotion for materials, emotion for money, emotion for physical relationship, emotion for social relationship, emotion for intellectual advancement and knowledge, emotion/longing for God or Goddess (spirituality): for most of us, our entire life we suffer from hunger or thirst for all these emotions strongly, except for the last one. I owe to you, Sri Sri Ramakrishna for instilling in me longing for deep spirituality.

The love that you have for your biological parents and siblings is because of two reasons: firstly, because of the genetic affinity (you share 50 percent of each of your parent's genes); and secondly, microbial affinity (you share common microbes because you consume the same food, use the same space, furniture, linens and so on).

A husband and wife have no affinity in these two respects, when they get married and start living together. Even after living together since 1965, we don't share any genes as we're from two entirely different families. After we live together for some time, we start sharing microbes. So REAL LOVE between husband and wife is SPIRITUAL LOVE based on the spirit of service and sacrifice (model: Sri Sri Ramakrishna and Ma Sarada Devi).

Therefore, your love for your biological father, biological mother, biological brother or biological sister, according to scientific school is SELFISH LOVE. This is Mother Nature's selfishness.

(Read: Richard Dawkins, Selfish Genes, London: Oxford University Press, 2016.)

Amazingly, your genes and microbes are agents of *maya* (delusion).

Why this Book

(The Background)

"'We are all mentally ill', said the abbot of Amaravati Monastery with a smile. It was an extraordinary declaration, but I knew exactly what he meant."

*[**James Kingsland**, Siddhartha's Brain: The Science of Meditation, Mindfulness and Enlightenment, London: Robinson, 2016, p.13.]*

Sri Sri Ramakrishna, at certain times, used to roll on the ground like a *Sufi* devotee; at some other time he would scream 'Ma' 'Ma' trying to get the attention of the Divine Mother; sometime he would be found sitting on the branch of a tree behind the temple, like a big baboon, displaying an artificial tail; sometimes he could be found with a bamboo on his shoulder walking on the ground with a thumping gait; at other times you'll find him singing with his melodious voice and dancing most rhythmically; you might also find him acting in the role of a gopi dressed and ornamented like a woman; at other times, you may find him with nothing on his body – moving like a naked naga sage. You would've never found him immersed in continuous meditation like a cave-dwelling monk. He would, at times, be busy learning the *Tantra*; you may find, at other times, Thakur taking lessons in *Vedanta* or *Vaisnava Shastra*. He would move from Christianity to Islam, from Sikhism to BaulOlogy and may be to 'Kartabhaja' also. So diverse was his *sport (leela)*!!

Those who did not know the 'real' Ramakrishna, used to call him 'mad'. But, as a matter of fact, he was the only person who was mentally healthy, the rest were all 'mad'. Some were mad for money, wealth, property, and prosperity, someone else for physical pleasure – sex, some others for loving relationships, a few others for prestige, status, name, fame and authority. All these are needs and desires covered under the Russian-American psychologist's popular *Hierarchy of Human Needs,* (Reference 1) taught in all courses of psychology, sociology, industrial management and business administration, except for his highest one which he had called 'self-actualisation' which my way of expressing is 'flourishing by discovering and knowing yourself'.

Rani Rashmoni (Reference 2), founder-owner of the Dakshineswar temple, came into the hall where the basalt image of Goddess Kali is installed, sat in front of the goddess by the side of Sri Sri Ramakrishna, asked him to sing a devotional song – but as the Saint started singing, within a few minutes, she became inattentive and could not escape the sight of Ramakrishna's *third eye* (Reference 3). Ramakrishna gave her a gentle push and said: "Even here in Goddess's room, your mind is engaged in the thoughts of a court case related to your property". The Rani was amazed: how Ramakrishna could read her mind? Wasn't it her transient madness? The person who is sane, in the truest sense, could catch it on the spot.

Rani Rashmoni was actually engaged in the DMN ('Default Mode Network') (Reference 4) of her brain. Empty brain, no doubt, is the devil's workshop. This devil is not the one that we read about in religious stories. This is the devil of 'madness'. Actually, when the brain is empty – it does not have any meaningful work to do, the DMN of the brain gets switched on. When the DMN is activated, random, unorganised thoughts appear on the mental screen – thoughts mostly related to the past failures and setbacks and future uncertainties. Our pre-historic hunter-gatherer forest-dwelling ancestors had good use for their brains' DMNs to plan for their provisions -where food will be available and can be acquired without much hassle, based on their past experiences. That utility of DMN has been lost once the human species got more organised at the dawn of civilisation; it has, ever since, been the devil's workshop. The most effective way to get rid of this devil is to fill the empty brain with God thoughts, chant god's name, or count the beads of a divine rosary. God kills the devil and saves the person with a task-disengaged brain. Sitting even in front of the Great Goddess, Rani Rashmoni could not control her brain's DMN and showed signs of madness.

Most of my working life, I have spent with such mad people in different corners of India, in our neighbouring countries: Nepal, Bhutan and Bangladesh as well as overseas – not so frequently though. These mad people consisted of big businessmen, top industrialists, first generation successful entrepreneurs, CEOs, presidents, vice-presidents, general managers and members of the entire management and supervisory cadres. Some of them were quarter mad, some half, a few others three-quarters, and a rare few almost full mad. And, in that population I had to interact with, included people with different proportions of madness. I will share with you two examples of almost totally mad businessman. One of them had his corporate reception and waiting hall walls adorned with framed photos (very large) of himself with celebrities like the Presidents, Vice-Presidents and Prime Ministers of India and the Chief Ministers and Governors of the State where he had his corporate HQ. This is an example of corporate narcissism (Reference 5) (I wouldn't know if Sigmund Freud or Carl Jung would have called it by any other name, References 6 & 7). The co-owner of a Rs. 5,000 crore cement industry (headquartered in New Delhi) called me for a very private meeting in his Calcutta Regional Office. All along the almost one-hour meeting that we had, I found him counting beads on a rosary with both his hands laid on his lap. From time to time, his deep sigh was accompanied with an almost inaudible 'Aum' chant. He opened up to me to say that he was having such a nervous breakdown that he chartered a helicopter to bring his family guru from Hardwar who had suggested him to do continuous japam and chanting. But, what was the root cause of his problem? There was no coordination between the departmental heads of his giant cement plant and they were all in competing rather than the cooperating mode. Whether I could cure their madness? When the personal ego reaches its peak, people get into a competitive than a co-operative mode. 'Ego' is one of the 'Six Enemies of the Mind' (Reference 8). In a team, the spirit should be 'We', 'Us', 'Our' – not 'I', Me', 'My'. The sign of madness is when the Plant Head will say 'My Plant'. From the word he uses, you can make out that he is a victim of corporate madness.

I thus spent over forty years trying to convert 'I', 'Me', 'My' to 'We', 'Us', 'Our'. I had to design effective 'team-building' and 'peak performance' management games and exercises to suit the culture. That was a most eventful era of my life. I earned my 'feel good' brain chemical 'Dopamine' ('D') by lessening (if not, totally curing) the degree of madness.

While researching on *Avatar* Ramakrishna Paramhansa, I was amazed to see how skilfully he would handle a few things. One of those was his 'Self-management' – how would he control himself whenever there was an external stimulus that would make him earn 'D' effortlessly. That skill must have been in him, innate, as an *Avatar*. The other was how amazingly, without any excess in anything, he would build a bridge of lasting trustful friendship with someone he was meeting for the first time. It is a part of 'Man Management'. He used to say quite often in Bengali: "*Amake roshe boshe rakhis Ma*" (In English: "Mother Goddess, please keep me always in 'good feeling' but under your strict control" – '*rosh*' represents 'D' and '*bosh*' represents 'control'. I had learnt these strategies by reading books, attending workshops & development programmes, interacting with luminaries like Prof. Bohdan Hawrylyshyn, PhD (1926–2016), former Director of the International Management Institute (IMI) at Geneva Switzerland (Reference 9) and Prof. Peter Drucker, PhD (1909–2005), Clarke Professor of Social Science and Management at the Claremont Graduate University in Claremont, California, USA (Reference 10). I took lessons from Prof. Hawrylyshyn at IMI-Geneva where I was spending a very short sabbatical in the late 1970's. I interacted privately with Prof. Drucker at the 1978 World Management Congress where I was a Rapporteur, and, of course, from my personal experience. Now, I am learning anew from the 'Soul' of a mystic – Sri Sri Ramakrishna Paramhansa. I feel, I am sitting at his golden feet.

For generally wise, talented, learned people, there is no respite from such madness, just like there is no respite for them from ill health, diseases, ageing and death. Those who have '*divya bhava*' (that is, 'spiritual inclination') in them, they are exceptions as those life circumstances do not affect them, as they are not guided by their 'gross bodies' – instead, they are totally under the control of their 'subtle bodies'. They are much beyond body consciousness.

According to the principles of Tantra, there are three types of *bhavas*: '*poshu bhava*', '*nara* or *veera bhava*', and '*divya bhava*'. (Reference 11). Those belonging to the first two groups would certainly behave madly, as it is in their nature. Externally, although they may look and appear civilised, internally they are still primitive. Are kings, queens, princes and princesses free from burning desires – do they not suffer from madness from time to time? Of course, they do. Prince Gautama Siddhartha was not free from desires and cravings which would have been readily met by his parents. So, he was not free from the kind of madness that we are talking about. Once he became Gautama Buddha, he was totally free from such madness, mentally totally healthy, and really wise. (Reference 12)

The kind of desire-linked madness that I am talking about, the neurotransmitter that is responsible for it, is called Dopamine ('D'). (Reference 13). It is one of the few main neurotransmitters that our nervous system has. It is released when we 'feel good'. Half of it is produced and released in the 'reward circuit' of our cranial brain – the brain between the two ears; and the balance half is produced and released from the neurons of the 'gut brain' – the 'enteric nervous system'. 'D' provides you with physical comfort and pleasure (from body massage, physical courtship (including kissing & cuddling) procreational & recreational sex, eating, drinking, urination, defecation) and so on. It also provides you with mental satisfaction and 'eureka' feeling and makes you euphoric when released in good quantities (Reference 14). You can earn 'D', according to your preferences, by listening to music; by singing or playing music; watching a dance performance or a drama, or movie; dancing, performing in a drama or acting in a movie (when you perform as well as when you receive appreciation); listening to a talk; attending the lecture of a great teacher or professor; giving a talk (including earning post-talk praise); reading a good book; searching for an information and getting it; getting engaged in social sites like Facebook, Instagram, Twitter and Linked In. In addition, we earn 'D' whenever we 'win' in any competition (don't forget that it is a 'reward chemical') – clearing a test or examination, succeeding in an interview and getting a job, earning a higher responsibility with a raise, promotion to a prestigious post, even when buying a new apartment, fridge, modern furniture or a car. And of course, ongoing for a date, getting engaged and eventually married and getting a kid. The whole life is a Dopamine Game. We survive on 'D' and live for 'D'. So, just like we have hunger for 'food', in the same way, we have 'Dopamine Hunger' (Reference 15); and this craving for 'D' makes us MAD.

Our 'Dopamine Hunger' is increasing with the speed of socio-economic progress and fast advancement of science & technology. So, the degree of madness is also increasing due to the presence of 'Dopamine Hunger' itself and also for the 'Unsatiated Dopamine Hunger'. My natural conclusion is, therefore, the rate of rebirth of souls with past life's 'Unsatiated Dopamine Hunger' is increasing. The womb-based 'Soul' in the foetus is also being influenced by the madness of the care-givers – especially of the mother, and a little less of the father – which is most alarming for the human society.

That Sri Sri Ramakrishna was an *avatar* can be confirmed from many instances of his life's history. I will share two most interesting ones here.

Gadadhar had gone to Nabadwip, Bhagawan Mahaprabhu Sri Chaitanya's birthplace. He had thought that if Sri Chaitanya was an *avatar*, there would certainly be some signs of his '*avatarhood*' in Nabadwip, where he was born. They toured all the sites but could not find a single one where there were some signs of Sri Chaitanya's '*Avatarhood*'. Being frustrated, he came back to the boat. When the boat had left the ghat and had travelled a little distance into the Ganges, Ramakrishna had an unique experience.

Two most handsome adolescent boys were seen moving through the air. Such handsomeness is rarely seen. Their skin was like molten gold; they had crowns of divine radiance encircling their heads. They had a charming smile on their face and were moving towards Ramakrishna. Ramakrishna shouted: "They have come, they have come!! Gaur-

Nitai!!" (References 16, 17 & 18). Just as he shouted, the boys came very close to him and entered into his body. He lost his senses in ecstasy. He would have fallen into the water, but his nephew who was his constant companion held him and prevented him from falling. That experience was good enough for him to get convinced that Nabadwip was truly the place where *avatar* Sri Chaitanya was born. And an *avatar's* spirit came to identify a living *avatar* – Sri Sri Ramakrishna.

On another occasion, Sri Sri Ramakrishna had been invited to a harisabha at Colootola in North Calcutta. Baishnabcharan, known to Ramakrishna, was reading from Srimad Bhagawad. Everyone present in the audience was listening intently, being totally engrossed. Ramakrishna arrived there and joined the audience.

The harisabha devotees had to imagine and believe that they were the *sevaks* (that is, servants) of Sri Chaitanya. They used to keep an *asana* in the centre and worship it imagining that Sri Chaitanya will listen to their call and appear. Nobody was allowed to infiltrate into that sacred zone.

While listening to Bhagawad, Ramakrishna lost his senses and suddenly he stood up and went into that sacred zone and stood on that very special *asana*. He immediately entered into *samadhi*. Real devotees realised that Ramakrishna had merged into the divine thoughts of Bhagawan Sri Chaitanya. This proves his '*avatarhood*'. Some got perplexed but remained calm, while a few others started chanting the name of Hari. Ramakrishna, hearing that chant, came back to his senses and began singing and dancing. After some time, when the *sabha* ended, Ramakrishna went back to Dakshineswar with his companions.

Sri Sri Ramakrishna, although he was an *avatar*, he had a 'gross body' where 'Dopamine Hunger' takes place. Unless you satisfy your body, what is the fun in life? Life becomes drab and pleasureless. Whenever there was any external stimulus for earning 'D', Ramakrishna had a special Self-management strategy (Reference 19) (almost 'miraculous') to control it.

In the area of Man Management (Reference 20), he had his own ingenious way of interacting with people, even with those, who had inflated ego-s, of allowing them to earn 'D' effortlessly so that very easily a solid permanent bridge would be built between the *Avatar* and the other person. How could a man from a rural background, almost illiterate, could perform such human bridge building is no less than a miracle. Spanning a river with a bridge made of steel or concrete is costly but much easier than building a man-to-man bridge of lasting relationship.

One main objective of this book is to expose my readers to some 'Subtle Sciences'. What we read in schools, colleges and universities – the 'mainstream sciences', I put those together under the group of 'Gross Sciences'. The 'miracles' that we experience cannot be understood in terms of common knowledge because those belong to the occult domain. Those can certainly be explained provided we look at them with the help of the 'Subtle Sciences'. Those miracles do not belong to the domain of MAGIC as many people still believe. Those can be performed by making use of the hidden powers of our brain which our hunter-gatherer forest-dwelling ancestors had developed to ensure their survival and safety. Today, since civilisation has given us enough handy tools and techniques for ensuring our survival and safety, we do not need them and they are lying dormant, as the yogis say, in the *kundalini* form at the base of our spine (Reference 21). Those can be revived by *yogic* and *tantric* practices. However, some people claim to be born with such extraordinary powers active since birth. One case that readily comes to my mind is that of the Israeli Jew, Uri Geller (Reference 22), who could even perform *psychokinesis* and *teleportation* (both doubtful though) (References 23 & 24), the former being changing the shape and size of a metallic object by psychic powers and the latter being shifting the gross body to a different distant location. We also read about many *autistic savants* (Reference 25) who have what is known as 'calendar memory'. *Calendar savants* can provide the day of the month within some particular range of years (watch the Tom Cruise & Dustin Hoffman-starring the 1988 American movie Rain Man) (Reference 26).

There is this controversial case of Swami Rama, an Indian yogi skilled in controlling his heart functions. This case was studied at the Menninger Foundation, USA, in the spring and fall of 1970 and was alleged by some observers at the foundation to have *telekinetically* moved a knitting needle twice from a distance of five feet. Although he wore a face-mask and gown to prevent allegations that he moved the needle with his breath or body movements, and air vents in the room were covered, at least one physician observer who was present was not convinced and expressed the opinion that air movement was somehow the cause. (Reference 27)

Anyway, these people were not *avatars* like Ramakrishna Paramhansa. Come, join me to delve deep into some of the extraordinary feats that he used to display which were far away from black magic (Reference 28) and voo doo.

References

[1] Saul McLeod, PhD "Maslow's Hierarchy of Needs", *Simply Psychology*, 24th January 2024.

[2] "Rani Rashmoni" – *Wikipedia.*

[3] "Third Eye" – *Wikipedia.*

[4] 'Default Mode Network' – *Wikipedia.*

[5] "Narcissism" – *Wikipedia.*

[6] "Sigmund Freud" – *Wikipedia.*

[7] "Carl Jung" – *Wikipedia.*

[8] "Arishadvargas (Six Enemies of the Mind)" – *Wikipedia.*

[9] "Prof. Bohdan Hawrylyshyn" – *Wikipedia.*

[10] "Prof. Peter Drucker" – *Wikipedia.*

[11] "The Three Temperaments (*Poshu, Naro* and *Divya Bhavas*)" – *Tantramarg*, 6th January 2016.

[12] "Gautama Buddha" – *Wikipedia.*

[13] "Dopamine" – *Wikipedia.*

[14] Whitney Ackers, "Is Dopamine Fasting a Way to Fix Your Brain or a Silicon Valley Fad?" *healthline*, 20th November 2019.

[15] "Brain hungers for dopamine" *Max Planck Gesellschaft*, 7th January 2019.

[16] "Gaura Nitai" *ISKCON Birmingham.*

[17] Dilip Kumar Ghosh, *Sri Sri Ramakrishna Punthi: Ek Akshay Shristi* (In Bengali), Kolkata: Sahityasree, 2023, p. 147.

[18] Dilip Kumar Ghosh, *Sri Sri Ramakrishna Punthi: Ek Akshay Shristi* (In Bengali), Kolkata: Sahityasree, 2023, pp. 148–149.

[19] Colleen Reilly, "Self-Management Skills at Work and Home", *Forbes*, 26th March 2024.

[20] "Man management", *Collins COBUILD.*

[21] 'Kundalini' – *Wikipedia.*

[22] "Uri Geller" – *Wikipedia.*

[23] "Psychokinesis" – *Wikipedia.*

[24] "Teleportation" – *Wikipedia.*

[25] "Savant Syndrome" – *Wikipedia.*

[26] "Rain Man" (movie) – *Wikipedia.*

[27] Elmer Green, Alyce Green, *Beyond Biofeedback* (2nd ed.) New York: Delacorte Press, pp. 197–218.

[28] "Black Magic" – *Wikipedia.*

CHAPTER 1

Avatar Sports

(A Few Instances of Sri Sri Ramakrishna's Unique *Leela*)

"One who has attained Paramhansa status, and has acquired the True Authentic Knowledge about the purpose of birth and life completely, he has already passed through all the lowly stages of a cremation ground attendant or a scavenger-sweeper to the higher social statuses of a landlord, a king, or even that of an emperor. Otherwise, how can he develop an apathy or a feeling of indifference towards the grossly materialistic world? His mind will be restless to see what he has not seen, what he has never experienced as yet."

[Translated from Bengali with some amendments; Rajib Sraban: Jugabatar Sri Sri Ramakrishna: Jana Katha Ajana Bishoy, Kolkata: Sen Brothers, 2024, p. 102.]

Avatar Sri Sri Ramakrishna's Sport (*Leela*) with 'Bliss Molecule' (*Anandamide*)

Ramakrishna used to be called 'Gadadhar' (short form 'Gadai') by his folks as his father had witnessed a dream, (while in Gaya) that 'Gadadhar', a form of Lord Vishnu was going to be born in his family as his son. Gadai, as a young boy, started becoming senseless at times. It was unlike any epileptic seizure as he would lose his consciousness whenever there was a stimulus, that would release 'D' inside his brain.

One of his very first fainting episodes took place when he was six or seven years old. One morning he was walking along a paddy field munching puffed rice. The sky was gorgeously clouded as if painted by a divine painter, and young Gadai was enjoying the scene immensely. All of a sudden, a flock of snow-white cranes came from somewhere and started flying across the sky. Against the dark black cloud, the flying snow-white cranes looked so ethereal that the scene acted as a trigger for Gadai to lose his consciousness. His unconscious body fell on the ground and the packet of puffed rice got scattered all over the place. It is not known for how long he was in that state but some passersby found him there and brought him home. Most interestingly, when he regained his consciousness and people showed great concern, Gadai said with a smile on his face: "On the outside, you see me unconscious, but inside I have a wonderful bliss." (Reference 1). Those who listened to the boy thought him to be MAD. As I have already told in the beginning under 'Why This Book (Background)' that Gadai was not MAD, the people who thought him to be MAD, were MAD.

I will share with you another incident of Gadai's fainting around the same period. The village boys of Kamarpukur used to love Gadai a lot. They wished him to remain with them always. These boys belonged to different castes. Some came from the family of oil traders, some were from low caste business families, and a few from an extremely poor background. They had the daily duty of taking their cattle to the field for grazing. Sometimes, they used to take Gadai along with them. Young Gadai enjoyed it very much and used to have a lot of fun. During such outings, Gadai felt as if he was young Krishna, the cowherd boy of Vrindaban. He could feel that one of his friends was Subol, another was Sudam, and a third one Basudam.

One day, while the cattle were grazing in the field, the boys were having puffed rice with Gadai, under the shade of a tree. They started playing with the puffed rice while eating by throwing it at each other. Gadai suddenly felt that he was in Vrindaban and he lost his senses. Finding this the boys were scared; they didn't know what to do. Some started sprinkling water on his face, some wiped his forehead with a wet cloth, some started calling him, but there was hardly any response. Some of the boys thought that he had been possessed by some evil spirit, and as they had been taught by the elders, they started chanting the name of Lord Rama. After some time, when Gadai regained his consciousness, the boys became relieved. When Gadai was asked by them why and how did it happen, he couldn't answer readily, but it was a blissful experience for him. There was no pain, no uneasiness in the body or in the limbs. (Reference 2)

Later on, whenever Gadai had such fits, his face used to glow with divine happiness. I wonder whether the boy got his first experience of release of the 'bliss molecule' *Anandamide* secreted inside his brain when the snow-white cranes flying across the dark clouded sky acted as the trigger? *Anandamide* (*'ananda'* – Sanskrit for 'bliss') is the first endogenous cannabinoid (exogenous is *cannabis*) identified in 1992 by Israeli scientists. (Reference 3). Years of investigative research on the popular exo-cannabinoid *cannabis* (or *marijuana*) which was Lord Shiva's favourite revealed that there are endocannabinoid receptors scattered in different parts of the brain which produces feeling of divine bliss when a specific endocannabinoid gets attracted towards and attached to those. The name *Anandamide* was taken by the lead researcher Dr. L. Hanus from the Sanskrit word *Ananda*, which means "joy, bliss, delight", plus 'amide'. (Reference 4). *Anandamide* exerts an overall modulatory effect on the brain's reward system. (Reference 5).

We all have *Anandamide* in our system, but those who have won the lucky gene have more of it and more frequently because they have less of an enzyme called FAAH, which deactivates *Anandamide.* It is a mutation in the FAAH gene that leads to more of the 'Bliss Molecule' *Anandamide* bathing the brain. (Reference 6). People having such natural genetic mutations do not need anything else to produce such 'calming effect'. In all probability, *Avatar* Sri Sri Ramakrishna was born with that lucky gene as he was divinely conceived. Singing, or listening to music along with or even without dancing can accelerate production of *Anandamide*; so those who can sing or dance have an advantage over others who do not. Here also Gadai was luckier than others in his age group.

Subsequent experience of *Gadai's* fainting (and *Anandamide* release) was when he was singing with his whole heart and soul poured into his sweet boyish voice. He was accompanying a group of village wives wearing saris with red border with baskets full of multi-coloured flowers. They were all travelling towards the temple of *Vishalakhsi Devi*, a little outside the village. Suddenly, Gadai became so absorbed in the song that tears started flowing from his eyes and, soon, he lost his senses. Having witnessed Gadai's fainting, the village women came running and started caressing him on the forehead. "What is the matter with you?", one lady asked. No response came from Gadai as he was unconscious; instead, some indistinct sound came from his voice. Some started sprinkling water on his face; but there was no effect at all, only an indistinct sound came from him. Gadai's companion Prasanna suddenly had a brain wave. He wondered whether *Devi Vishalakshi's* spirit had entered into Gadai's body. (Such occurrences were common in the rural culture in that era). So, Prasanna started addressing young Gadai as if he was *Devi Vishalakshi*: "Oh My Goddess *Vishalakshi*, please don't be annoyed with this young, innocent soul. *Devi Vishalakshi*, please bring him back to senses." Most astoundingly, as many times Prasanna uttered the name of Goddess *Vishalakshi*, Gadai's face shone with a pure smile. And, after a few such occurrences, Gadai came back to his senses. And all the village women started expressing their deep gratitude towards the Goddess and paying respect to Her. They started feeding Gadai with fruits and sweets. (Reference 7)

So, the switching circuit was fully identified and discovered now. Whenever there is an exposure to some divine, spiritual, ethereal or highly aesthetic experience be it a sight or a sound, Gadai's *Anandamide* circuits will be switched on and he will lose his senses. To bring him back to senses, one has to give him another divine input in the form of a prayer, or a mantra, a devotional song, or just an *AUM*.

The next episode of Gadai's *Anandamide* experience occurred during his performance of the role of *Lord Shiva* in his village. The seniors of his village had decided to put up a play where they were looking for someone to play the role of *Shiva*. After some thoughts, they selected Gadai for the role for his acting talents. On getting this news, Gadai's friend Gangabishnu, along with his associates, started dressing up Gadai for the role. In the dressing room itself Gadai started getting into a different mood thinking that he was real Shiva. The moment he entered the stage, the audience started offering their pronam to him and started shouting "Hara Hara Mahadev!" A few started chanting the '*Shivastotra*'. Gadai stood absolutely still with tears flowing out of his eyes, and then he fainted. He could not act in the role for which he was dressed and made up. Some of his friends carried his unconscious body home. The ladies at his home – his mother and aunts started blowing the conch shell to help him regain his consciousness.

It reminds me of a Baul song, which says:

> "Get immersed in your own soul
> and witness the beauty there
> It is the permanent abode of
> the eternal God!" (Reference 8)

After this incident, Gadai's moodiness increased whenever he used to think about or listen to songs about gods and goddesses. At times, he also used to lose consciousness. Such *Bhav-Samadhi* had, in course of some time, came under his own control. He could get into it at will. Some people used to think Gadai had a streak of madness in him. A few others would think that he had been possessed by some evil spirit. But, in reality, it was not so. He was born different, born with a different soul. (Reference 9)

In *Tantra*, this is called *Divya Bhava* (divine state of mind) when the mind transcends the mundane worldly level and enters into a divine domain. (Reference 10)

Gadadhar: Face-to-Face with Gender Bipolarity

'Gender Bipolarity' is a sign of true spirituality. In Hinduism, it is the *Shiva-Shakti* combination. By Gender Bipolarity, I do not mean that one should have both the genitals physically. The Soul should have both the components that makes a pair – masculine and feminine. Both these qualities make a true 'God' or a 'Goddess'. Both Lord Shiva and Goddess Kali are ideal examples.

Young Gadadhar's character was an ideal combination of *purusha* and *prakriti*. When he was under the spell of the *prakriti* part of his personality, he used to have a peculiar desire. He used to mutter to himself: "If I were to be born again, I would like to be born in a Brahmin family as a most pretty child widow with thick long hair". He used to look at the white clouds flying across the sky: "Lord Krishna would be my husband – full of true love for me. There would be enough provision for my simple food, clothes and shelter. There would be a land for farming adjacent to my hut. There would be healthy cows to be milked in the cowshed. I will milk the cows myself. And, at the end of the day, after finishing all the work, I will cut thread on the spinning-wheel. In the evening, I will light the earthen lamp near the *tulsi* tree and then make sweets from the cow milk. I will make delicious sweets to feed Lord Krishna and shed tears until He eats those from my hand. Being moved by my anxiety, Sri Krishna will come to my hut. Every day, he will come without anyone noticing him."

Gadadhar, in his early teens, used to be a regular visitor to his neighbour the Pyne family's house. Pyne had seven sons and eight daughters. Gadai used to play with all of them in the inner precincts of their big house. Pyne's cousin Durgadas was against his adolescent daughters attending Gadai's narrating stories from the *Puranas*. Once Gadai told him: "Can you protect your daughters by not allowing me to enter your house? If I wish, I can see and listen to everyone inside your house." There was a spirit of challenge in his voice.

One late evening, Gadai dressed up like a young village girl and went to Durgadas's house posing as if she had come to the village market and it became so late that she cannot get back home. She was looking for a night shelter. His make-up and acting were so perfect that Durgadas couldn't recognise him and, out of kindness, allowed her to go inside and stay with the women folk there. By the time, he was well-settled there as a young village maiden having chats with the women in the house and enjoying delicious snacks, Gadai's brother Rameshwar came looking for him. On the way, he got the information that Gadai was in Durgadas's house. When he came to Durgadas's and called Gadai's name, Gadai replied back and came running. Everyone was awe-struck to find the immaculate skill with which Gadai had made himself up as a girl and acted in the female role. Durgadas's ego was shattered.

Gadai started playing both male (Sri Krishna/Ram) and female (Sri Radhika/Sita) roles with equal skill and started training village youngsters – both boys and girls how to act. During such activities, he would get into a different mood which will take his mind into a different world, away from reality.

This is how, Gadadhar crossed his teenage and stepped into his youth by being fully aware of both the genders and performing both in male and female roles. Was it due to the presence of a half-man/half-woman (*Ardhanarishvara*) psyche in his personality? (Reference 11)

I am sharing with you, here, one instance where he was totally into the female gender, his male existence was totally out of his mind. It was evening time – time for *arati* puja of the Goddess. Ramakrishna had lost the sense of his male body. In all his expressions – verbal as well as non-verbal, it was too difficult to make out whether he was a male or a female. His entire disposition was conveying a message – that he was either the maid ('dashi') or the friend & companion 'sakhi' of the Goddess, for all times.

The Goddess had occupied his life-force ('prana') and mind ('mana'), his everything. His living and working were all for the Goddess. He had a beautiful smile on his face; his postures and gestures were all very feminine. He had put on a beautiful silk sari, gifted by Mathur Babu, and had worn it like a woman. Mathur's wife had ornamented her with all her jewellery. So, all dressed and decked up like a pretty woman, he could not be recognised even by Mathur Babu when he was standing with the ladies at the time of sandhya *arati* and fanning the Goddess with a chamar. (Reference 2)

Throughout his life, there has been a combination of male and female characteristics in Gadadhar. Due to this combination of two opposite propensities, on the one hand he was extremely rational, looking for a cause for every effect. On the other hand, he had a very soft side of his personality like an affectionate compassionate woman. However, he was quite balanced and never went to any extreme.

Nevertheless, there might have been exceptions though. There is one instance which has been documented: "Thakur told Sri M in private – I'm telling only you; others must not know. When I am in the mood of *prakriti* (female), I feel a very strong desire to kiss and hug a *purusha* (male)". (Reference 13)

Sri Sri Ramakrishna's *Leela* with His *Aura*

Aura is the 'energy field' with which an individual is surrounded. It is a speculated subtle emanation around the body. Every living organism has an *aura*, even a leaf has. These *auras* can be seen by clairvoyant people. *Clairvoyance* is an extra-sensory special power which enables one to see the *aura* of living objects. It is an entirely 'spiritual' concept which the psychics feel is the *subtle body ('Sukshma Sarira')*. Many of the conventional mainstream scientists do not accept it. However, spiritually most advanced persons have a most powerful aura with which they can perform healing, transform people's nature, offer special 'rewards' to those who deserve. (References 14 & 15) Let me share two good examples of how Sri Sri Ramakrishna used his *aura* to bring about changes in people. (References 16 & 17)

Once Thakur had gone to Bhadrakali village near Uttarpara which was on the other bank of the river, to listen to a *kirtan* performance. The *kirtaniya*s started their performance when he reached there. With the sound of *kirtan*s, the atmosphere became most solemn.

In the meantime, a pundit by the name of Brahmobrata Samadhyai met Paramhansa and expressed his intention to discuss scriptures with him for some time. Thakur asked his devotee Mahima Charan who had accompanied him to start the discussion, as Mahima Charan was well-trained in Hindu scriptures. They started discussion about 'duality' (*Dvaita-bad*) and 'non-duality' (*Advaita-bad)*. Samadhyai was totally against 'duality' and he was quoting points, from the shastras, confirming the validity of 'non-duality'. Half an hour got past and it was found that Mahima Charan was not able to defend himself. That was when Ramakrishna joined in the discussion. However, Samadhyai started ruling out Thakur's arguments by quoting from different authentic Hindu scriptures.

Suddenly Thakur stopped and begged to be excused as he wanted to go to the toilet. He took his other companion Ramlal with him. He had a self-talk: "Oh! I find this man to be very argumentative. It's OK, but there is a polite way of putting his points forward."

He soon returned to the discussion session where Samadhyai was waiting for him. Thakur, before he sat down, touched his body and smook him a little softly and said: "Please repeat what you're saying a little while ago". Samadhyai was speechless. He had lost all his power to argue any more. (Thakur apparently had infused a little bit of his *aura* into Samadhyai's body which had transformed him totally.) The pundit was watching Ramakrishna in utter surprise as he could get a feel of his stupendous spiritual power. He was wondering how Ramakrishna had transformed him. Brahmabrata lost all his cognitive powers when he experienced REAL Ramakrishna. He said with a powerless voice: "Sir! I've nothing to say. Whatever you've said is true and I accept it whole-heartedly." What Samadhyai had not realised earlier because of his vanity, because of the darkness created by his ego, he now realised most clearly by a simple soft touch on his body by the *avatar*. That is how, the *avatar* used to play his sport *(leela)*. (Reference 16)

I'm sharing another example of how Thakur used his *aura*. One brahmin, by the name of Nrityagopal Goswami came to meet him when, in an ailing state, he was staying in Balaram Bose's house. Nrityagopal used to teach in a college in Dacca. Paramhansa greeted him most respectfully as he had seen the brahmin was dressed like a good Vaishnava. In the hot weather, it was so warm that Thakur sitting in his small room, at that time, was using a hand fan to get some air. The brahmin saw this and thought that how good it will be if I could be of some service to the saint by fanning him instead of he fanning himself. Thakur could read his mind from his body language and gave the fan to him. The brahmin started fanning him with full dedication and utmost sincerity. Ramakrishna was very happy with his dedicated service and, in a *bhava* mood, kept one foot on the chest of the man who could immediately feel the power of the *avatar's* blessing. Tears started pouring out of both his eyes. The atmosphere was most spiritual. After some time, when Thakur got into a half-awake state, he told the brahmin: "Say Sri Krishna Chaitanya – Say Sri Krishna Chaitanya". When Nrityagopal repeated the name three times, Thakur came back to his normal senses and started talking to others who were present. (Reference 17)

How Ramakrishna Used to Handle His 'Dopamine Hunger'

'Dopamine' ('D') is the most important messenger substance of the 'reward system' of our brain. Whenever we 'feel good' or have a 'pleasurable experience', 'D' is released. Most amazingly, half of the total 'D' available in our system is released in the 'cranial brain' (the brain between the two ears) and the balance half is released in the 'gut brain'—the digestive system.

Sri Sri Ramakrishna, although he was an *avatar* and thus guided by his '*subtle body*' ('*sukshma sarira*') and 'subtle consciousness' generally (being in *bhav* most of the time when alone), he had the '*gross body*' ('*sthula sarira*') which had its own 'Dopamine Hunger'. (References 18 & 19)

For Ramakrishna, the 'D' release in his cranial brain was totally under control. He had developed his own, shall we say, 'servo control' or 'thermostatic control' (or may be was born with it) for the 'D' release. Whenever there was an external or internal emotional stimulus triggering a 'D' release, he would automatically lose his consciousness or go into a short spell of *bhav samadhi* (don't confuse with *savikalpa* or *nirvikalpa samadhi*) from which he would wake up when someone nearby would chant an 'aum' or any other mantra. For common people, it was a phenomenon shrouded in mystery. This was Thakur's own ingenious way of 'Dopamine Fasting' ('DF'). (Reference 20). 'DF' involves abstaining from activities which may over-excite or over-stimulate you like sexual thoughts, sights or provocations. Such 'DF' had occurred in Ramakrishna's life when once Mathurbabu had left him alone in a prostitute quarter all by himself; on another occasion, when two prostitutes were thrown into his small room in Dakhshineswar who started making vulgar gestures; and, once more, when one of his disciples had taken him to a garden party full of provoking young women.

Low 'Dopamine' ('D') levels can manifest in several symptoms, the following two amongst those were most noticeable in the case of Sri Sri Ramakrishna: (1) indifference about things that people generally enjoy; and, (2) lack of interest in sex. (Reference 21)

However, once it had happened with his own wife, Sarada Devi. Young Sarada had come to stay in Dakhshineswar from her own village via her in-laws' home in Kamarpukur. One night, she was sleeping in the same bed as Sri Ramakrishna. She was asleep and Paramhansa was awake. He looked at her youthful body and said to himself that the situation might have been planned to allure him to have physical relationship with his wife. This thought was the trigger for his sudden fainting and getting into '*bhav samadhi*'. (Reference 22)

[Later on, on one occasion, the Paramhansa had said to his devotees: "Even when your wife is with you in the same household, if you're continuously driven by your conscience and true science, then you've managed to establish yourself in real brahma or 'cosmic energy'. He, who looks at both the male and female genders as manifestations of the same Cosmic Soul or the 'Universal Self', and treats both accordingly, attains authentic knowledge. Those who look at the two opposite genders separately, although they may be following a spiritual path, they may remain far from true spirituality."]

However, as a consequence of his 'Dopamine' ('D') hunger control through control of his senses, his desire for 'D' was related only to his 'gut brain'. Occasionally, all of a sudden (possibly when his 'D' reserve would be depleted), he would have a terrible appetite and he would simply turn MAD, if he could not be provided with something to eat even puffed or curd rice. There were several occasions when this had happened in his own village Kamarpukur, his in-laws' village Jairambati and, of course, in Dakshineswar. Once, in Dakshineswar, his hunger pang was so acute that he consumed a whole box full of sarpuria, an Indian sweet preparation – a quantity meant to be eaten by 4/5 people. Low 'D' function results in stronger cravings for food which may well result in 'binge-eating'. Sri Sri Ramakrishna was of a lean constitution, so instead of his occasional over-eating leading to excess belly fat, he used to suffer from gastro-intestinal problems. (Reference 23)

While served with good food, he used to become like a child, not bothering about what others will think about his childishness. Ma Sarada used to get embarrassed, at times, due to Thakur's food fetish. It so happened that while giving sermons to his disciples and devotees, he would just disappear to go to the Nahabat (where Ma Sarada used to stay) to enquire what all are being cooked. He used to avoid any discussion on this topic if anybody asked any question.

One day, Sarada Devi asked him and he confided in her. He said: "In order to live in this mortal life, we have to satisfy our needs. A dying person has no needs. I have conquered all my needs. This is the only need that is making me live. The day you'll find me refusing the food that you've cooked for me and I am so fond of, you'll know that my time has come to leave this body." Ma Sarada got confused but didn't bother Thakur.

The D-day came after seven long years when they had shifted to Cossipore. Ma Sarada had cooked his meal and took it to him. Paramhansa was lying on his bed. Finding Sarada with the food, he turned his face and said that he would not like to have anything. When Sarada asked him, he told her to remember what he had said seven years earlier. Sarada started crying. Within the next 2–3 days, Ramakrishna breathed his last. (Reference 24)

Sri Sri Ramakrishna and His 'Oxytocin' Hunt

Devotion is not based on logic, but on faith and trust. And, the neurochemical for 'faith' and 'trust' is 'Oxytocin' ('O'). Therefore, there is a direct link between 'devotion' and 'O'. A typical Indian is more prone to devotion than he is guided by knowledge. It is emotion, not thought, that motivates him. The effect of emotion is, in any case, first noticed by the vibrations of the heart.

Sri Krishna had said to Arjuna: "O Arjuna! Be devoted to me, become my devotee, worship me, bow to me. By doing this, you will attain me. Without devotion, salvation is not possible." (Reference 25)

Avatar Sri Sri Ramakrishna thus was an 'Oxytocin' ('O') Hunter. In the treatise on 'Devotion' – *Bhakti Shastra*, there is a mention of 19 (nineteen) *bhavas* or moods.

There are 5 (five) primary relationships, leading to different *bhavas*: neutrality (*shanta*); servitude (*dasya*); friendship (*sakhya*); parental (*vatsalya*); and, conjugal (*madhura* or *madhurya*).

There are 7 (seven) secondary *rasas*: laughing (*hasya*); having wonderful visions (*adbhuta*); entering into a chivalrous relationship (*veera*); experiencing pity (*karuna*); feeling anger (*roudra*); and, experiencing ghastliness (*bibhatsa*) and devastation (*bhayanaka*).

The 7 (seven) steps to reach the end point of prema (or, 'true love') are: sraddha (faith & trust); enthusiasm for *sadhu sanga* (company of devotees); *nistha* (steadiness in service); *ruci* (taste); *asakti* (attachment to Lord); *bhava* (genuine ecstatic emotion); and, *prema* (true love).

So, altogether you have 19 (nineteen) *bhavas* or moods.

When prema ('true love') is mixed with the processes of devotional service, it is called '*vibhava*', '*anubhava*', '*sattvika*' and '*vybhichari*'.

Symptoms of 'anubhava' can be divided into 13 (thirteen) categories: (1) dancing; (2) rolling on the ground; (3) singing; (4) yelling; (5) jumping; (6) making loud noises; (7) yawning; (8) heavy breathing; (9) not caring for public opinion; (10) discharging saliva; (11) roaring laughter; (12) unsteadiness; (13) hiccupping. (Reference 26)

There are nine-fold devotional services. These are: hearing (*sravanam*); chanting (*kirtanam*); remembering (*smaranam*); serving the Lord's lotus feet (*pada sevanam*); deity worship (*arcanam*); praying (*vandanam*); serving as a friend (*sakhyam*); and, complete surrender (*atma nivedanam*).

If you go through Sri Sri Ramakrishna's entire life, you will find that, knowingly or unknowingly, he had followed the entire spectrum of practices, as laid down in the *Bhakti Shastra*.

Ramakrishna's Forays into Cremation Grounds

While at Kamarpukur, the villagers, at times, used not to find Gadadhar anywhere. He will just disappear into wilderness. He would visit, especially, the two cremation grounds which the villagers used to avoid unless they were compelled to go there to cremate somebody. These two cremation grounds were: *Bhutir Khal* and *Budhui Morol*, respectively located in the south and north-east corners of Kamarpukur, Ramakrishna's ancestral village. Gadadhar used to sit there for his meditation as the places were desolate and ideal for sadhana as you can remain undisturbed. Goddess Kali takes the form of Smasahan Kali in cremation grounds, her left foot instead of the right one, placed on Lord Shiva's chest, and all her accessories and other things held on opposite hands, compared to her normal disposition. (References 27 & 28)

It has been documented by Akshay Kumar Sen, author of the *Ramakrishna Punthi*, that Gadadhar used to carry with him pots full of sweets not for his own consumption (I'll tell you about whose consumption the sweets were meant, a little later). Thakur's elder brother Rameshwar, finding him not returning home till late at night, would go near the cremation grounds and shout his name. Gadadhar, hearing his call, would warn him: "Dada! Please don't come any closer as you might get possessed by ghosts who will harm you."

By the side of the cremation ground near Bhutir Khal, he had planted a Bel tree; and he used to meditate under the ancient Aswath tree. Thakur used to do his sadhana by the side of the Tulsi forest.

Now, remember that we are only 10% human. There are nine microbes for every living cell in our body and brain. (Reference 29)

When a person dies, the body's microbial guests start eating the body which is getting decomposed. It happens when the person is buried underground with or without being laid in a coffin. What happens when the corpse is burnt instead of being buries, as in Hindu culture? The microbes leave the dead body in anticipation of being burnt with the corpse; and they start looking for live or dead bodies where they can take shelter. So, Hindu cremation ground is a place filled with all kinds of microbes – good and evil, sober and aggressive. The Tantriks and Aghoris, when they ride on a cadaver, they collect the dead person's microbes which may add to their microbial diversity which is good – both for physical and mental health.

Ramakrishna used to carry pots full of sweets possibly to feed the stray dogs and foxes as well as the wandering microbes trying to enter his body. Being an *avatar*, he was aware of the existence and conduct of the microbes and used to take appropriate measures to prevent them from taking shelter in his body.

How Ramakrisna Gave Young Narendranath (Who Later Became Swami Vivekananda) His First Experience of 'Dopamine Fasting' ('DF') by Sharing a Slice of His Soul

Narendranath was just eighteen years of age and was a fiery youth. He had many questions always popping up on his mind regarding the existence of God, and so on. One day, somebody told him that there is a mystic, his name is Ramakrishna, he would have all the answers to Naren's questions.

Naren got worked up. He collected all his vigour and went straight to meet Ramakrishna face-to-face. He asked him without delay: "You say God, God. Where is the proof that there is God?" Ramakrishna smiled at him and said: "God is in front of you.". Naren requested him: "Can you make me experience God in whatever way it may be?" The Paramhansa said: "Do you have the courage to experience Him?" Naren was a very courageous young man; he said: "Yes, of course!". Ramakrishna lifted his leg and put his foot on Naren's chest. Naren felt as if he was electrocuted. Ramakrishna had shared a very thin slice of his luminous Soul with young Naren which took his consciousness away and gave him a smart 'DF' experience.

God is *nirakar* (formless, empty, vacant) as well as *sakar* (having a form, full) like we have a subtle body (sukhsma sarira) and a gross body (sthula sharira). When your mind is exposed to emptiness (devoid of all external as well as internal stimuli), you are in a 'Dopamine Fasting' ('DF') brain state. That is when you experience *nirakar brahma.* (Reference 30)

I have put it under Sri Sri Ramakrishna's Self-management Miracles as it is impossible for someone like you or me to transplant a slice of our Soul into someone else's Soul. (Reference 31)

My other interpretation of Naren's sudden transformation is as follows. According to *Sankhya Darshan*, Lord Shiva who is lying underneath the standing Goddess Kali, has no power to act, no power to consume and enjoy (that is, *bhoga*). He is alone, desireless, but he is fully conscious. He is the *Purusha*. Goddess Kali is *Prakriti*. She makes the *Purusha* carry out tasks. What kind of tasks? Mainly, the task of 'creation'. *Prakriti* is capable of consumption and enjoyment, but she is not conscious. Creation is possible only when Lord Shiva, the *Purusha*, gets merged into Goddess Kali, the *Prakriti*. Goddess Kali's right foot is placed on the chest (near the heart) of Lord Shiva, thus making a circuit between the heart of the *Purusha* and the 'Left Brain (LB)' (representing action) of *Prakriti*, charging the *Purusha* for destruction of all delusions (*maya*), leading to positive action. (References 32 and 33)

When Naren wanted to see God and figure out how it is, Ramakrishna imagined that Naren was *Purusha* (Shiva) and Goddess Kali worked through him, making him to represent *Prakriti*. Naren, as *Purusha* had consciousness but was devoid of any power to act. Ramakrishna brought Kali's power into him being Kali's child and made Naren wake up from his delusive slumber and become positively active. Naren was transformed.

A Short Note on Sharing a Few Slices of the Soul

According to the 'Three Bodies Doctrine' of Hinduism, the human being is composed of three '*bodies*' or '*sariras*'. They are often equated with the five '*koshas*' ('sheaths') which cover the *atman*. This doctrine is most essential in Indian philosophy and religion, especially Yoga, Advaita Vedanta, Tantra and Shaivism.

The most complex amongst the three is the '*Karana Sarira*' or the '*Causal Body*' contains the impressions of experience and is merely the cause of the gross and the subtle bodies. It is *nirvikalpa rupam* – "undifferentiated form". '*Karana Sarira*' has many interpretations but my perception of it is that at this stage the consummation of the *atman* with the *paramatman* is reached and the search for the highest '*Purusa*', that is, of '*Ishvara*' ends. It is not the atman or the Soul itself. A *yogi*, I understand, can experience it in the deep sleep state where intelligence or buddhi becomes dormant and all concepts of time fail.

The '*Sthula Sarira*' or the '*Gross Body*' is the material, physical, mortal body where all signs and symptoms of growth, development, ageing and ailments show up. For example, Thakur Ramakrishna was afflicted with cancer in his '*Sthula Sarira*' ('*Gross Body*') whereas his '*Sukshma Sarira*' ('*Subtle Body*') was unaffected. It is composed of all anatomical parts and physiological systems which take from and give out to the external world. It represents the waking state and the *anatman*.

The '*Sukshma Sarira*' or the '*Subtle Body*' is the body of the mind and the vital energies, which keep the physical body alive.

Together with the '*Causal Body*', it is the transmigrating soul or *jiva*, separating from the '*Gross Body*' upon death. (Reference 34)

The '*Sukshma Sarira*' or the '*Subtle Body*' has all the five sense organs and also the five organs of action, the five-fold breath (*pancha prana*), '*Manas*' (the 'emotional mind' and the 'desires') and '*Buddhi*' (the intellect, the discriminating wisdom) which manifests itself in the waking state. The 'dream state' is a distinct state of the '*Sukshma Sarira*'.

In modern medical practice, before a donor's organ or a part of it is transplanted into a recipient's body, lot of biological matching exercises are done so that the donated organ is well-matched with the recipient's body and there is no complication and, at the worst, rejection. (Reference 35). Coming back to our 'The Doctrine of the Three Bodies', it is the '*Sthula Sarira*' or the '*Gross Body*' is involved in the transplantation procedure while the '*Sukshma Sarira*' or the '*Subtle Body*' certainly gets affected before and after the transplantation.

I have developed the concept of Transplantation of One or More Slices of the Soul in my recent scholarly work on Sri Sri Ramakrishna. He being an *avatar* had the capability to transplant slices of his golden soul. (Reference 36). It was a part of his Self-management Miracle. His Soul was his own property, it was possible only for himself to share it with another person. For you and me, it is an unimaginable and impossible act.

Golden Souls descend on this planet from time to time when there is a rising crisis of spiritual values.

Sri Sri Ramakrishna's Subtle Body in Belur Ramakrishna Temple to Experience 'Dopamine Effect' ('DE') 'Dopamine' ('D') is released when you have old happy memories.

Swami Somesewarananda writes: (Reference 37)

"I was posted at Belur Math then. My evening duty used to be in the Ramakrishna temple. After the *sandhya arati*, my task was to clean up Thakur's bed room. The clothes, shoes, books and other few belongings of his are preserved on the first floor of the temple. From there the stairs go up to the second floor where his bed room was located. There was nothing much there. A cot, a pair of slippers, and so on. After the *arati*, after dusting the stairs and the rooms, I had just started mopping the floor, meticulously, suddenly I felt as if someone had entered the room where I was working. By 'entering', I don't mean that somebody had entered through the door. I could suddenly feel the presence of somebody – I could feel the person's energy vibrations; could feel the presence of a big man. I could feel that the man was 9 to 10 feet tall. He was standing near the cot. In the squatting posture, I looked back but couldn't find anyone. I started mopping the floor again. Within a few seconds, I got the same feeling. Somebody was there. I stood up – looked around. Came out of the room to check if someone was there on the stairs. But, alas! Nobody was there. Again, I started my mopping work. Again, I had the same feeling. I was not scared but the incident appeared most mysterious to me. The vibrations could be felt distinctly. I was alone on the second floor. There was nobody on the first floor. There might have been three or four sadhus and brahmacharis on the ground floor.

I came down alone to the first floor. I couldn't find anyone there. Again, I went up to the second floor and resumed my work. And, had that feeling again!! There was no fear or tension in me, only some uneasiness. I could feel, most distinctly, somebody's presence in that room where Thakur used to rest. I tried to ignore the whole incident, but simply couldn't. It was so clear that it was impossible to count it out as hallucination. The whole time that I was working – almost 20 to 25 minutes, I could feel the presence most distinctly.

Later on, I shared this experience with Dhiren Maharaj who was on worship duty in this temple for many years. He burst into laughter and said: "You're a lucky person. Many people had the same experience there. Thakur is still present even now!!'"

My question is: why does Ramakrishna still visit and spend time in the quarters where he lived for many years? Are the past memories still there? In one way, his belongings are the only things that are familiar to his wandering Soul; all the people are new and thus not familiar. Or, does he come to get the vibrations of the invisible microbiome which, by now, might have multiplied manifold with successors of the microbes that used to reside in his belongings when he was alive (because he misses them as he felt the presence of God in everything)? Being in touch with the things that were his and he had used in the past regularly, will have a 'Dopamine Effect' ('DE') on him. Or, is it to ensure that his belongings are left entirely on their own because even a soft touch may result in some subtle energy carrying negative vibrations of his cancer-ridden diseased body moving to the person who had touched the stuff?

There could be one more possibility (hope it is not too far-fetched). While Ramakrishna's Soul remained in space, a portion of his Subtle Body was still retained in the things that he would use regularly. And, whenever, any human being came into his room, that Subtle Body used to get active from its stationery position. The Subtle Body is large in size – larger than the Gross Body. Nature is compelled to squeeze the Subtle Body to facilitate the activities of the Gross Body. Since the Subtle Body is not 'gross', it can move anywhere and through anything that it likes.

A most remarkable occasion was when Swami Vivekananda had gone up to Sri Sri Ramakrishna's bedroom to do his meditation on the day he left his body for the higher space. He had sat on the floor of the Paramhansa's room, possibly touched his bed and the furniture but nothing has been reported whether he had also felt the presence of someone. (Reference 38)

Sri Sri Ramakrishna's Subtle Body to Provide 'Oxytocin' ('O') to His Direct Disciples

Any living creature, including humans, needs its *consciousness* for fulfilment of its twin basic objectives of living: 'survival' (including 'food' for survival and survival from predators; and 'replication' for passing on its genes to the next generation. For a monk who has taken *sannyas*, it is only fulfilment of the first objective that matters, as he has no place for the second one in his life.

The incident that I'm talking about took place years after the Paramhansa had passed away and when some of his disciples had gone on a pilgrimage.

Swami Brahmananda and Swami Turiyananda had been travelling somewhere in North India and living on madhukari (begging for daily food as is customary for a *sannyasi*). They were passing through a very difficult time, were not getting any alms so there was nothing for them to eat. They were compelled to fast. After a lot of search, Turiyananda could locate some esculent stem ('*kachu*' in Bengali) which he boiled and both of them had it. Swami Brahmananda, after eating that boiled root vegetable had developed severe sore throat which could be relieved only with the help of drops of lime. Swami Turiyananda started looking here and there and praying to Sri Ramakrishna so that he could get some lime. There were lemon trees, but all had leaves but not a single fruit. Finally, he could locate one lemon tree which had only one fruit hanging. Turiyananda Ji thanked Sri Ramakrishna and offered it to Brahmananda who consumed fresh lime juice and got relief from his sore throat.

These two monks were starving for two days and Brahmananda was so upset that he remembered Sri Ramakrishna and said: "You had taken us out from our households and had assured us of food, clothes and shelter. But you're not keeping your promise. If you do not organise food for us as soon as possible, we will leave *sannyas* and go back to householder's life." That was night time and they slept in empty stomach.

They woke up very early in the morning and went for their morning ablutions and bath to a local river. A ram-bhakt *sannyasi* came running towards them. When he reached near them, he said: "I'm so glad that I've found you. I'm a ram-bhakt *sannyasi.* I've been wanting to offer bhog to Lord Rama for many years, but he had not been responding to my prayers. Only very early this morning, he said that please keep the *bhog* ready, I will have it and also invite two *sannyasis* whom you'll find near the bank of the local river, early in the morning. That is why I'm here to invite you. Please come with me." The two Ramakrishna-bhakts accompanied the Ram-bhakt *sannyasi* who had cooked some *bhog* which they all consumed after offering to Lord Rama.

Sri Sri Ramakrishna's wandering soul had received the complaints of Brahmananda and organised their food through the Ram-bhakt *sannyasi.* He provided 'Oxytocin' ('O') – the trust molecule to two of his direct disciples. (Reference 39)

References

[1] Rajib Sraban, *Jugabatar Sri Sri Ramakrishna: Jana Katha Ajana Bishoy* (In Bengali), Kolkata: Sen Brothers, 2024, p. 29.

[2] Dilip Kumar Ghosh. *Sri Sri Ramakrishna Punthi: Ek Akshay Shristi*, (In Bengali), Kolkata: Sahityasree, 2022, p.25.

[3] D. Piomelli, "Anandamide: (Endocannabinoids)", *Science Direct*, Quoted in: Encyclopaedia of Biological Chemistry (Second Edition), 2013.

[4] "Anandamide" – *Wikipedia.*

[5] Maria Sherma *et al.*, "Brain activity of anandamide: a rewarding bliss?" *Acta Pharmalogica Sinica*, March 2019, Vol. 40, No/Issue 3, pp. 309–323, Published online on 26th July 2018.

[6] Richard A. FrIedman, "The Feel-Good Gene", *The New York Times*, 6th March, 2015.

[7] Rajib Sraban, *Jugabatar Sri Sri Ramakrishna: Jana Katha Ajana Bishoy* (In Bengali), Kolkata: Sen Brothers, 2024, pp. 33–34.

[8] Rajib Sraban, *Jugabatar Sri Sri Ramakrishna: Jana Katha Ajana Bishoy* (In Bengali), Kolkata: Sen Brothers, 2024, pp. 35–36.

[9] Rajib Sraban, *Jugabatar Sri Sri Ramaktishna: Jana Katha Ajana Bishoy* (In Bengali), Kolkata: Sen Brothers, 2024, p. 37.

[10] Akshay Kumar Sen, *Sri Sri Ramakrishna Punthi*, (6th Edition), Kolkata: Udbodhan, p. 15]

[11] Rajib Sraban, *Jugabatar Sri Sri Ramakrishna: Jana Katha Ajana Bishoy*, (In Bengali), Kolkata: Sen Brothers, 2024, pp. 41–44.

[12] Dilip Kumar Ghosh, *Sri Sri Ramakrishna Punthi: Ek Akshay Srishti*, (In Bengali), Kolkata: Sahityasree, 2023, p. 135.

[13] Rajib Sraban, *Jugabatar Sri Sri Ramakrishna: Jana Katha Ajana Bishoy*, (In Bengali), Kolkata: Sen Brothers, 2024, p. 116.

[14] "Aura (paranormal)" – *Wikipedia.*

[15] "Clairvoyance" – *Wikipedia.*

[16] Dilip Kumar Ghosh, *Sri Sri Ramakrishna Punthi: Ek Akshay Shristi* (In Bengali); Kolkata: Sahityasree; 2023, pp. 198–199.

[17] Dilip Kumar Ghosh, *Sri Sri Ramakrishna Punthi: Ek Akshay Shristi* (In Bengali); Kolkata: Sahityasree, 2023, pp. 209–210.

[18] "How Does Dopamine Affect the Body", *Healthline*, 2019.

[19] Heiko Backes, "Brain hungers for dopamine: Neurotransmitter release regulates our eating behaviour", *Max-Planck-Gesellschaft*, 7th January 2019.

[20] "What do you know about dopamine fasting", *Medical News Today*

[21] Elizabeth Plumptre, "The Most Common Low Dopamine Symptoms", *verywellmind*, 19th May 2024.

[22] "Mind Blowing Incident of Sri Ramakrisna's Samadhi – Swami Saradananda on Master's......", *Hindu Monk*, Video on YouTube.

[23] "The Link between Dopamine and Binge Eating", *Eating Disorder Hope.com*, 29th March 2024.

[24] "Thakur Ramakrishna Keno Eto Khete Bhalobasten?" Bengali Video Presentation in YouTube, Thakur Ma Swamiji.

[25] "Devotion" – *Wikipedia.*

[26] "What are the different kinds of *Bhakti Rasa/Bhava*?" *Quora*

[27] Dilip Kumar Ghosh, *Sri Sri Ramakrishna Punthi: Ek Akshay Shristi* (In Bengali), Kolkata: Sahityasree, 2023, p. 66.

[28] "Smashan" – Video Presentation in Bengali on YouTube by Nrishingha Prasad Bhaduri.

[29] Alanna Collen, *10% Human: How Your Body's Microbes Hold the Key to Health and Happiness*, Glasgow: William Collins, 2015.

[30] "Swami Vivekananda's Samadhi" – sadhguru # shorts, video presentation.

[31] Siddhartha Ganguli, *Goddess Kali, God Thoughts Sri Sri Ramakrishna and A Few Slices of Sri Sri Ramakrishna's Soul*, Noida: Allied Publishers Pvt. Ltd., 2024.

[32] "Kali" – Video Presentation in Bengali in YouTube by Nrishingha Prasad Bhaduri.

[33] "Smashan Kali" – Video Presentation in Bengali in YouTube by Nrishingha Prasad Bhaduri.

[34] "The Doctrine of the Three Bodies" – *Wikipedia.*

[35] "Organ transplants" – *healthdirect.*

[36] Siddhartha Ganguli, *Goddess Kali, God Thoughts, Sri Sri Ramakrishna and A Few Slices of Sri Sri Ramakrishna's Soul,* Noida: Allied Publishers Pvt. Ltd., 2024.

[37] Swami Someswarananda, *Amar Sannyas Jiban o Belur Math* (In Bengali), Kolkata: Girija Library, 2021, pp. 22–23.

[38] "Swami Vivekanander mrityur din sakal theke daha kara porjonto ki ki ghotechilo", (In Bengali) Video presentation on YouTube by Panch Nama.

[39] 'Ek Asadharan Satya Ghatana' (In Bengali) YouTube Video Presentation by 'Spiritual Bulletin'.

CHAPTER 2

Sri Sri Ramakrishna's Brain

"Mother *('Ma'* in Bengali)! Who are you to have given me a space in your golden womb? You are certainly not an ordinary mother!!" Ramakrishna used to say this often to his biological mother Chandramani Devi as he knew very well that he was an *avatar*!".

—Translated & adapted from the Bengali book by Dilip Kumar Ghosh, Srimo O Sri Ramakrishna Sangha: Ek Nibir Jogasutra, Kolkata: Sahityasree, 2022, p. 27.

"It is I who have watched over thee, life after life, in the tenderness of many mothers! See in my gaze, the two black eyes, the lost beautiful eyes, thou seekest!"

*—**Paramhansa Yogananda**, Autobiography of a Yogi, www.holybooks.com, 1946, p. 18.*

Sri Sri Ramakrishna's Brain: Infusing Life into a Lifeless Goddess

Sri Sri Ramakrishna was engaged as the priest in the temple of Goddess Kali *(Bhabatarini Ma)* in Dakshineswar. 'Is it a living goddess or just a lifeless one?' He was very much bothered with this question. And, since he was not just an ordinary professional priest but an *Avatar*, he wanted to explore. He once took a small piece of cotton and held it near the deity's nostrils to check whether she was breathing or not. And, most surprisingly, the cotton started moving to indicate that the deity was a living goddess.

Henceforth, whenever he would enter into the temple and look at the basalt stone deity, he would find her taking a living form in front of him. He would experience that the deity's consciousness is responsible for the whole world's consciousness. Goddess Kali is present everywhere in Her all-protective form. (Reference 1, pp. 176–177)

On another occasion, he had the desire to worship Devi Durga. It used to be seen that whenever whatever worship or *sadhana*, Sri Sri Ramakrishna wanted to do, *Bhabatarini Ma Kali* would make it happen. Both of them had a perfect understanding like what exists between a mother and her child. It so happened that a Durga idol emerged from the Holy River Ganges. The image walked towards Thakur and stopped near him. He worshipped Her to his heart's content. Once the puja was over, the image walked back to the river and got immersed by itself. Ramakrishna became suspicious. Did it really happen or was it just a delusion? As he was wondering, he found the Goddess's firm footprints on the ground and he was convinced. (Reference 1, p.176)

Exogenous psychedelics can produce such hallucinatory effects in the brain. They help grow, maintain, and repair brain-based neurons. DMT (Di-Methyl-Tryptamine) is a plant extract which is an effective exogenous psychedelic. Humans and animals also produce DMT in small quantities under certain conditions in the brain as well as in the gut, leading to intense visual and auditory psychedelic experience (References 2, 3, 4 & 5). There is no data available whether Ramakrishna's brain used to release endogenous DMT from his *Pineal Gland (PG).* My speculation is that it was not unlikely as *PG* is the brain's doorway through which the wandering *Soul* enters into the foetus exactly after 49 days (7 weeks) of pregnancy. Ramakrishna's *Soul* came from divine sources as has been documented. *PG* is also known as the *Third Eye.*

DMT is called the *Spirit Molecule* due to the intense psychedelic experience.

Sri Sri Ramakrisna's Brain: Its Magnetic Power

Sri Sri Ramakrishna: "Just see! A peacock had been fed with a little dose of opium exactly at 4 O'clock in the afternoon. The very next day, the bird arrives there at 4 pm sharp – the opium has done its job to make the bird addicted."

Sri M's (author of *Sri Sri Ramakrishna Kathamrita*) self-talk on listening to Ramakrishna's words: "He is absolutely right. I go home – my body moves but my mind still remains here, in the saint's room. I become too eager – when shall I see him again and feel his presence – when shall I hear his mesmerising and motivating words again. Someone is pulling me to him with a strong magnetic force. Even if I recollect that I have to go somewhere else, all other forces lose. I get ready and go to him who has transformed me totally."

—Translated in English and adapted from the Bengali book "Srimo O Ramakrishna Sangha: Ek Nibir Jogasutra" by Dilip Kumar Ghosh, Kolkata: Sahityasree, 2022, p. 7.

Sri Sri Ramakrishna's Brain: What Powers He had to Infuse Life into a Goddess Made of Stone

Soon after Sri Sri Ramakrishna took over, from his elder brother Ram Kumar, the responsibility of worshipping Goddess Kali at Dakshineswar after his initiation into the *shakti* cult by Kenaram Bhattacharya, the basalt stone image of the deity began becoming alive. Perhaps Thakur had shared a few slices of his luminous soul to enliven the Goddess. Besides, Thakur himself was a sculptor and proficient image-maker himself. As a result, he could feel the life-force vibrating in every nook and corner of the idol's body.

Let us take the case of a modern image-maker, Manjunath Achar of Kolar district, South India (References 6 & 7). According to him: "A boulder doesn't look like a piece of stone for me but like an image of a mythological character. I visualise figures that could be carved out of the stone. I set out to work once there is clarity in my thoughts."

About the Kali of the Dakshineswar temple, when the news spread, hordes of people from all over the place started coming to visit the deity and they all acclaimed that the Dakshineswar Kali was totally different from other Kali idols installed in different temples. Everyone started wondering how it has been possible generate that difference.

The truth possibly is this. Ramakrishna became the priest of Goddess Kali not just to perform a brahmin's job. He was most anxious to know the REAL Kali at the core of the carved basalt as he had been making clay Kali idols in his village Kamarpukur. He wanted to talk to Her, interact with Her. He wanted to hear Her voice. The stone-carved Goddess could feel his urges, resonate with the vibrations of his longings, and became alive – eager for interaction.

Gadadhar was certainly very different from ordinary commonplace priests. And this difference, if measured, we could have seen, that it worked out to be of 360 degrees.

Sri Sri Ramakrishna's Brain: Its 'Error Detection Circuit'

One of the areas of our brain that is known to be important for 'self-monitoring' is the 'Medial Frontal Cortex' ('MFC'), but how exactly this process works and how it fails when it does not work, remains poorly understood. There are specific neurons or 'brain cells' known as 'Error Neurons' in the human MFC that signal the detection of errors. Those of us who are very sensitive to any error due to negligence or absent-mindedness (not 'ignorance') have most active 'Error Neurons'. (References 9, 10 and 11)

Now, let us take the case of the Hindu gods and goddesses. Those gods and goddesses who are very particular about their dress, jewelleries, accessories and articles held in their hands would, I presume have very strong, sensitive and active 'Error Neurons'. Amongst the popular deities, I presume, Lord Shiva and Goddess Kali are the only two exceptions. They are callous about how they are dressing up and what they are wearing in their body. In Ramakrishna's Kamarpukur home, Lord Rama (Raghubir) used to be worshipped. Raghubir is well-dressed. Ramakrishna's father Khsudiram saw Lord Vishnu in his dream who said that He will be born as Khsudiram's son. Lord Vishnu is immaculately dressed and ornamented. Ramakrishna's mother had experienced a radiance of light entering into her womb from the Shiva temple, near which she was standing. That must have been a slice of Lord Shiva's soul. Lord Rama and Lord Vishnu, both being well-dressed and attired have strong 'Error Neurons'. Lord Shiva, a slice of whose soul had entered into the womb of Chandradevi and made her pregnant is most callously dressed like a yogi – a hermit, thus having dormant 'Error Neurons'. This, I speculate, had made young Gadai, born out of Chandradevi's womb, least fussy and pernickety. Coming from a very orthodox Brahmin family, he was least concerned about and affected by religion, caste, creed, and community. He used to play with boys of different castes and communities and have food in different households. During his sacred ceremony, he took food not from any brahmin motherly lady but from Dhani Kamarni who had belonged to a very low caste.

During the inauguration of the Dakhshineswar temple, hundreds of people were invited and there was a big feast, but young Gadadhar, who had just been brought to Kolkata from Kamarpukur by his elder brother Ramkumar who had been appointed the chief priest in the temple, did not touch the sumptuous food in the temple precincts; instead had one pice worth of sweetened puffed rice. Many scholars have written that this was because Rani Rashmoni had belonged to a very low caste. But, as a brain scholar, I feel that conclusion is wrong. He did not take the temple food because there was the rich lady's ego ('rajasik' according to *Triguna* and '*naro bhava*' according to *Tantra*) attached to it which was some kind of a contamination and he was sensitive to it. So, perhaps, Sri Sri Ramakrishna's 'Error Neurons' were influenced by the '*tamasik-rajasik-sattvik*' and '*poshu-naro-divya bhava*' principles of the *Vedic Triguna* and the *Tantrik Tri-bhava* concepts. (References 12 & 13)

Ramakrishna Paramhansa was least conscious about his clothes and, there were times, when he would have nothing on at all while loitering in the bowers behind the Dakshineswar temple.

Throughout his entire life, you will notice that, Paramhansa was least sensitive to religion, community, caste and creed, and more sensitive towards purity and true humanity. He voluntarily got indoctrinated in all main religions following the rituals of each and came up with the '*Jato Mat Tato Path*' ('There are as many routes as there are opinions') slogan which is very famous.

I'm sharing two soul-touching stories, from the *Avatar's* life, with you.

The first one is regarding a man named Rasik who used to work in Dakhshineswar as a sweeper. He belonged to the untouchable community. He used to sweep the temple daily and used to find so many people of all strata of life were coming to visit Ramakrishna, pay respect to him and take his blessings. The temple used to attract them because of the Paramhansa – the God in flesh-and-blood.

Sometimes he is singing, sometimes dancing, at other times talking to or listening to his devotees and visitors and, at times, meditating. Rasik had never met any such peculiar person in his life as, to him, he was unlike any other person that he had seen or known. He used to stand in front of Thakur's room or wait by the side of his path when he came out of his room; but Thakur was so engrossed with his own thoughts, that he hardly noticed him. Rasik was extremely keen to get his blessings directly from him. He devised an ingenious strategy. He went and waited in front of the room where Sarada Devi used to stay. And, at an opportune moment, he shared his wish with Ma Sarada.

One day, when Ma Sarada was with the Paramhansa, she told him about Rasik's keen desire to get his blessings. Within a day or two, when Sri Sri Ramakrishna was returning from the Ganges after his bath, Rasik was cleaning up the place and, finding Thakur, he was about to clear out from his path when Thakur himself came forward and told him: "I'm told that you want to witness God. Come, come close to me. I'll show you God." Thakur moved forward and hugged him closely. Rasik was, as if, struck by a lightning. He got true blessings from the Godman. The storehouse of the love-compassion-trust chemical 'Oxytocin' (Reference 14) got opened up inside Rasik's brain and a slice of the *Avatar's* soul entered into the untouchable's body. He became purified and blessed.

The second story goes like this.

Inside the temple, one day Paramhansa suddenly saw the face of a beautiful woman peeping out from behind the Goddess. He looked around but could not find anyone. When he came out of the temple, he could see an exquisitely pretty woman standing.

"Who are you, my dear? Just now, I saw your face behind the image of the Goddess inside the temple."

The woman was about to touch his feet to take his blessings, but he wouldn't allow it. The woman was also adamant.

Thakur said; "You are my Mother, how can I take your *pronam*?" The cloud inside the woman's mind got burst into incessant tears – all her sins got washed off in a moment. Her name was Ramani, she was a prostitute, body-selling was her business. She has never received so much respect, such regard in her life so far. *Avatar* Ramakrishna restored her from the underground and lifted her up and, as if, placed her on the higher floor of a building.

Ramani went to Sarada Devi, told her everything, and wanted to touch her feet. She said: "Thakur has addressed you as 'Ma' – you are a most respectable relation of ours. How can I take *pronam* from you?" Ramani had brought some fruits and vegetables for Thakur and Ma Sarada, but was hesitant to offer those to her, she being an untouchable prostitute. Sarada talked to her most lovingly and took those offerings gladly promising to her that she will offer those to Thakur. The floodgates of the true love chemical 'Oxytocin' got opened inside Ramani's brain and she was a transformed person. (Reference 15)

Lord Jesus also used to cure lepers with his touch and transform prostitutes, but *Avatar* Ramakrishna's way of making socially unworthy and unacceptable people worthy and acceptable – was it any different? May not be, because all Godmen have some similar traits and streaks. (Reference 16)

'Oxytocin' promotes growth and healing. 'Oxytocin' is released through touch during hugging, embracing, body massage, and physical therapy and speed you on your way to healing. (Reference 17)

Sri Sri Ramakrishna's Brain: Three Stages of *Bhava*

The different types of *bhava* that Sri Sri Ramakrishna used to have, from time to time, were nothing but different *'Altered States of Consciousness' ('ASC')* (Reference 18).

At the onset of a light type of *bhava*, Thakur used to see a sight which was nothing but a haze, a foggy view. The second stage of Paramhansa's *bhava* was a wonderful experience. He used to witness clusters of fireflies vibrating like twinkling stars all around him. In the third stage, he used to find his surroundings radiant with divine light coming from the planets and stars. When he used to get merged into the ocean of light, he would lose his body consciousness and sense of time, place, and space. He used to get exposed to his luminous *soul*. One would have felt that a river has met with an ocean – some scholars have described it as an *'oceanic feeling'*. (Reference 19).

In a 1927 letter to Sigmund Freud, Romain Rolland coined the phrase *'oceanic feeling'* to refer to a sensation of 'eternity', a feeling of 'being with the external world as a whole', inspired by the example of Ramakrishna, among other mystics. (Reference 20)

Sri Sri Ramakrishna's Brain: Its 'Practical Intelligence' ('PI') Circuit

It is known to us that Sri Sri Ramakrishna was not interested in rote learning right from his boyhood. He was most irregular in his attendance at the village school. Later on, also, both his elder brothers, Ramkumar and Rameshwar could not make him interested in studies. Possibly because, his brain lacked an active and strong 'Academic Intelligence' circuit. However, when he was not in a spiritual mood, his brain's 'Practical Intelligence' ('PI') circuit became quite active. I'll share one example. (Reference 21)

It was almost autumn time in the Bengali calendar year 1262. In the Dakhshineswar temple, there was a very special arrangement for worship and offerings. In the afternoon, after offering *bhog-prasad* to the Radha-Krishna deities, the priest Khsetranath Chattopadhyay kept the Radharani Idol in her bedroom. Then there was a sudden accident while shifting the image of Lord Krishna. Due to negligence, the idol fell from the hand of the priest and one of its legs was broken. There was an immediate commotion amongst the priestly crowd and guests present. Everyone thought that it was a very bad omen. The right thing would be to immerse the broken image in the River Ganges and get a new idol. (Reference 22)

Although an order was placed for a new image, Rani Rashmoni's son-in-law Mathur Babu wanted to consult Choto Bhatchaj (Gadadhar was sometimes addressed by Rani Ma and Mathur Babu fondly this way) as he had a lot of respect for and confidence on him. Ramakrishna remarked in a most sarcastic way. "You have decided to immerse the broken idol in Ganges and get a new one. What would you've done, if one of Rani's son-in-laws had broken his leg? Would you have rejected him and got a new son-in-law?" Everyone was spellbound at Gadadhar's smart answer. After saying this, Gadai looked into Mathur's eyes with a naughty smile. He continued saying: "Will a new son-in-law be brought or would arrangements be made to get the present son-in-law's broken leg repaired?"

Mathur Babu had got the taste of Ramakrishna's 'Practical Intelligence' ('PI') already earlier. This time, he really got emotionally moved on hearing Ramakrishna's opinion. The people present there were also amazed at Ramakrishna's most intelligent response. On the one hand, they could not discard Gadadhar's argument; and, on the other, they could not go against what they had recommended earlier. They just kept quiet. And, after all, when Mathur Babu accepted it outright, they did not want to disagree.

When Mathur conveyed Gadadhar's opinion to Rani Rashmoni, she was also very impressed and decided to act accordingly. So, arrangement began to get the idol's broken leg repaired. Mathur was already aware of Gadadhar's image-making and sculpting skill, so naturally he assigned the task to Gadadhar without a second thought. On the request of Mathur, Ramakrishna got the broken leg repaired so meticulously, that nobody could make out that a broken part had been repaired. It looked like a new one.

After that incident, the priest who had been engaged to worship the Krishna idol lost his job and Gadadhar was assigned the responsibility. Gadadhar, while performing the worship, used to get so much lost that he used to get into the 'Flow Brain State' ('FBS') losing track of time, place, space and his 'I' feeling – the ego. (Reference 23)

Another very good example of Sri Sri Ramakrishna's 'Practical Intelligence' ('PI') is the set of strategies he used to recommend for handling people who are problematic for you. (Reference 24)

In the first group of people, he used to put those who will create trivial problems for you. For people in this group, he used to recommend the T-T-T strategy meaning 'Tolerate-Tolerate-Tolerate'; if you go on absorbing the problem and 'tolerating' without reacting, the problem-maker is likely to give up after some time as he would lose patience.

In the second group, he had put people who are aggressive and rude. For handling them, he had recommended the 'Threat' strategy; finding out some weakness and threatening the person that you will expose him.

In the third group, he would include people who are much stronger and more powerful than you. For handling such people, he had recommended a 'T-N' (that is, 'Tiger-Narayana') strategy. Since the other person is ferocious and vindictive (the 'Tiger' analogy), he shows respect to him from a distance (the 'Narayana' analogy) and avoid him.

Another striking example of Sri Sri Ramakrishna's 'PI' is 'Taka Mati, Mati Taka' saying (In English: 'Wealth is Soil, Soil is Wealth') which is often quoted. If you have lot of possessions including money and wealth, some people will hover around you for getting a share like bees hover around a beehive in search of honey. If you acquire a lot of fixed, movable and liquid assets, what will happen to those after you leave this planet, nobody knows. Your heirs might be already well-placed and inheriting your assets will make them too much wealthy. On the other hand, if your heirs are not well-to-do – they/some of them are just manging three square meals a day, the wealth inherited from you may lead to tax burden (property tax, wealth tax etc.). Sri Sri Ramakrishna had a very high level of 'PI' which prevented him from saving anything and building up assets. He knew that if he had any, there would be many takers who will come to him and it will interfere with your sadhana. When my father passed away, the fixed assets passed on to my mother who was still living; when she passed away the fixed assets came to me and my brother – but none of them had left any liquid assets as fixed deposits or savings in their banks. Was it Sri Sri Ramakrishna's plan?

Some Ramakrishna scholars feel that his illness was also his planned sport (*leela*). They feel that it was his strategy for finding out who were closest to him – those who did not leave him towards the last phase of his life. (Reference 25)

Sri Sri Ramakrishna's Brain: Another Demonstration of His 'Practical Intelligence' ('PI')

As Gadadhar entered into his teens, he used to get torn between two opposite thoughts. On the one hand, he had very strong emotional ties (that is, *maya*) with his widowed mother, his brothers and their families, his village friends & associates and other local acquaintances. On the other hand, he had his inner DRIVE to become a change-agent for which, he strongly felt, that he had been brought to this planet for some time – not just to lead a mundane life like most people.

However, to pursue the second alternative, he would have to sever his emotional ties and leave the family, relations, friends and associates at Kamarpukur and take up the life of a recluse, which appeared most painful for him – wearing saffron robes, chanting *mantras* in front of a sacrificial *homa* (fire), living on food collected by begging, and leading a secluded lonely life. Gadadhar was a very emotionally charged person. He shuddered at this thought. At the same time, he thought he would never be able to realise his DREAM if he could not cut off his emotional ties. Whenever he had such trains of thoughts, he could hear as if his mother was calling him: "Where are you, Gadai my son! Why don't you go to the puja room and check whether I've completed all arrangements? I might have missed something in a hurry." The innocent, helpless face of his nephew Akshay (who had lost his mother soon after childbirth as had been predicted by his elder brother Ramkumar) would flash on his mind's screen and both his eyes would be filled with tears. He murmured: "Let the life of a *sannyasi* go to hell!" Again, he thought that he was being too selfish and family- and clan-oriented. With that kind of bondage, he will never be able to translate his DREAM for a new world, a new society into reality.

He started looking for his fulfilment by strategically combining the life of a lonely recluse and that of a householder fulfilling his family obligations. This became a reality by the grace of Goddess Kali after he spent some years at the Dakshineswar temple, got settled, and the temple owners and others came to know his worth. The DOMAIN that he chose was not related to any particular religion but of SPIRITUALITY by combining slices from different 'key' religions of the world. So, that completed the DREAM-DRIVE-DOMAIN (3-D) cycle that successful entrepreneurs adopt. Sri Sri Ramakrishna had an entrepreneur's brain – not of a business or an industrial entrepreneur, but of a SPIRITUAL ENTREPRENEUR.

Sri Sri Ramakrishna's Brain: Some Extra Special Powers

Sometime after his elder brother Ramkumar passed away, Gadadhar started showing symptoms of lack of mental balance and everyone thought that he had developed a streak of insanity. Gadai's mother Chandramani got the news and brought him over to Kamarpukur for a change.

In Kamarpukur, like his earlier pre-Dakhshineswar days, he burst into cries saying 'Ma' 'Ma' like a little child and, while doing so, gradually lost control over his body. The teenager boy was like earlier, simple, innocent, pure, but his outburst of such cries had increased. He used to cry like a small child. He spent a few months with his mother at Kamarpukur and his health had somewhat improved.

However, there were some new developments. Sometimes, he will be missing from home and would go to the local cremation ground, as if he could feel the presence of spirits there. He will take some sweets and snacks which will all be eaten up by the stray foxes and invisible microbes residing there. Some days, he would spend the whole night there; he never returned home. His brother Rameshwar used to go to the cremation ground, wait at a distance, and call him by his name.

While Gadadhar responded, he used to ask him not to advance any further lest the evil spirits there would cause harm to him.

As time passed, Gadai's 'Ma' 'Ma' outbursts stopped. He used to take his bath and meals regularly like a most sane normal householder. He also used to perform his household duties most sincerely. Gadai's mother Chandra was very happy at her son's transformation. The other members of the household and his neighbours thought that he has been cured of his insanity. Nevertheless, his periodic absent-mindedness, moodiness and disinterest in all activities still persisted. His mother Chandradevi and brother Rameshwar both thought of getting him married.

One day, suddenly, something totally unexpected happened. Gadadhar went into a near-trance and suddenly said: "Go to Jairambati. Visit the house of Ram Mukherjee. You will find the girl there who is destined to be my wife. You don't have to search here and there. My marriage has been fixed long ago." Everyone was surprised as to how Gadadhar could say such a thing most firmly and confidently.

(They could not imagine that Gadadhar was not an ordinary person. He was born with some very special powers in his brain, which are not normally seen. And, this incident happened much before his *Tantrik* and other *sadhanas*.)

Gadai was not mad; he was DIFFERENT. Chandradevi had a dream experience after a few days later after Gadadhar had returned to his Dakhshineswar temple duties. Lord Krishna appeared in her dream and consoled her with the words: "Don't worry. Your son is NOT MAD. It happens to him under spiritual spells. He has a divine soul unlike a common lad of his age. Don't misunderstand him."

A few days later, in the temple precincts, Mathur Babu had a very special experience. Ramakrishna was walking along the corridor – going and then coming back. Mathur was watching. Mathur came and fell at his feet and said: "You are very special. When you are going away from me, I feel Lord Shiva is passing; and, when you're coming back, I find Goddess Kali is approaching me." So, apparently, Gadadhar had special powers in his brain to produce visions in others' minds. (Reference 26)

Sri Sri Ramakrishna's Brain: The Two 'I's

Inside the human brain, there is an 'I', the good side of which is that it protects the individual from all threats and obstacles. And, its bad side is that it makes the person totally closed, a slave of prevailing socio-religious customs and practices. Common people have this 'I', which I would call the 'Small I'. It is extremely conscious about its surroundings; and, it is guided by the culture of shame, disgust, and fear.

There is a 'Big I' which is just the opposite. It is in the divine domain where shame, disgust and fear are non-existent. For Sri Sri Ramakrishna, such a divine domain used to be provided by both Lord Shiva (*Purusha*) and Goddess Kali (*Prakriti*). Both of them are callous and careless about covering their respective bodies. Sri Sri Ramakrishna had imbibed such habits while in the *bhava* (mood) of that divine domain. He would take out his sacred thread which was the sign of his birth caste as a high caste brahmin. At times, he would be careless about covering her bare body with something. His soul having imbibed slices of Goddess Kali's and Lord Shiva's soul would create such uneasiness in his body that he will have irritation all over – thus being unable to keep any clothes on. There was complete soul-to-soul identification between the divinity and the devotee. This is, what I call, true devotion. Since he claimed that he used to communicate with the Goddess, I speculate that, he used to get a silent message from Ma Kali quite often. The message was "Remain in *bhava*". Perhaps she wanted him to remain like a child – without any small 'I' – without anything on, if he wanted her to be his mother. Thus, for Ramakrishna, she was not an ordinary goddess, she was his Mother Goddess. And, because he regarded the Goddess as his mother, he used to regard all women as his mother – human goddesses, whether it be his own married wife Sarada, or the prostitute Ramani who came to take his blessings. These are typical signs of an *avatar*, to my mind.

An *avatar*, can never be recognised and understood by people who are rigidly orthodox and routinised, guided only by the scriptures and religious customs and practices. Take the case of Haladhari, who was Gadadhar's cousin, on his father's side. Haladhari was very well-read in the Hindu shastras and he used to have serious academic discussions with the naga monk Totapuri when he was in Dakshineswar. Haladhari had a very active 'Small I' and he would expect Ramakrishna to have a strong and active 'Small I' like him.

In the Bengali year of 1272, Haladhari was relieved of his duties at the Radhakantajiu temple when Ramakrishna's nephew Alkshay had taken his place. Ramakrishna had an intimate relationship with Haladhari. They used to interact on different topics of mutual interest. However, Haladhari had developed no idea about who Ramakrishna really was. He was very suspicious about his peculiar behaviour as any normal person would become. Very frequently, when under the spell of a *bhava*, Gadadhar used to take off his sacred thread and throw it away. Haladhari did not like it at all. He took Hriday into confidence and told him: "Hriday! Gadai often gets undressed. He throws away his sacred thread. These are all signs of his disrespect towards his Brahminical status. Does he want to give away his higher caste? If that is true, then what a shame it would be."

While Haladhari was talking to Hriday, they could hear Gadai's voice coming from the temple. He was screaming 'Ma', 'Ma', like a madman. A child may cry for the mother, but if a grown-up man cries like that, is it not a sign of madness, Haladhari thought. Hearing such screams, Haladhari had stopped talking. He was most unhappy at his cousin's such abnormal behaviour. He remembered the name of Radhakantajiu and said: "What has happened to him that he dares to indulge in such indecent behaviour?" He told Hriday: "Your uncle listens only to you. Please persuade him to behave decently. Ramakrishna's anxious voice did not stop. It continued to come from the temple. Haladhari told Hriday, "You must have found something really special in him. Otherwise, how could you have remained inactive and unresponsive."

Haladhari used to get disgusted when Gadadhar used to dress like a female when he had *Madhura Bhava*. He used to criticise him directly on his face. Ramakrishna used to have different visions about God. You don't have visions when you are not under the influence of a *bhava*. He used to get the message from his Goddess, repeatedly – "Remain in *bhava*. This will help you in your future role of a teacher of mass education". While in *bhava*, he used to lose his 'Small I' – his selfish ego. His body, brain, mind and ego all used to get converted into nothingness. He would see and feel only the Mother Goddess, Goddess Kali. He used to get the message from Goddess Kali: "Remain in *bhava*." – which means even if the 'I' feeling goes, it does not remain as *Nirguna*. It becomes the 'Giant I' – the 'Universal Self' and one has to follow its instructions for further advancement. (Reference 27)

Sri Sri Ramakrishna's Brain: Poor Self-Management

Immediately after having stayed in the '*nirvikalpa samadhi*' domain of the brain from time to time for six months, six months of illness that followed had somewhat helped to bring Ramakrishna's mind habituated to travel down to the level of body consciousness that had disappeared. First, let me try to explain. Please be with me. We own only one body with different parts – organs, systems and extremities. But we have two brains; a third has also been discovered a few years ago. In the body, wherever there are clusters of brain cells or neurons, we regard that portion as a brain.

We have the 'cranial brain' – the brain between the two ears, which has 8,500 to 10,000 million neurons in it. This is the First Brain. The Second Brain has been identified a couple of decades ago in the digestive system. This, also known as the Gut Brain, has more than 500 million neurons. This most complex neural network outside the First Brain operates within the gastro-intestinal (GI) tract and controls the digestive functions. The Third Brain is an intricate network of several types of neurons, neurotransmitters, proteins, and support cells similar to those found in the First Brain. Its elaborate circuitry enables it to act independently of the 'cranial brain' – to learn, remember, and even feel and sense. Discovered in 1991, this 'little heart brain' is composed of approximately 40,000 neurons. So, the heart has its own 'cardiac nervous system' like the 'enteric nervous system' in the gut. (References 28, 29 & 30)

However, most interestingly, we are only 10% human. For every one of our cells, there are nine microbes – bacteria, fungi and other micro-organisms who are our guests. Our gut alone hosts 100 trillion of them. Recent research findings say that microbes run our bodies and becoming healthy is impossible without them. (Reference 31)

These gut microbes thrive on the food that we consume. If we have a regular balanced dietary habit (carbohydrates, proteins, fat, vitamins & minerals, roughages, probiotics), then the entire population of our gut microbes remain healthy and happy as different species of microbes like different types of foods. A healthy gut microbiome prevents disorders of the digestive system such as acidity, gas, wind, indigestion, flatulence, constipation, loose motion, amoebiasis, and 'Irritable Bowels Syndrome' ('IBS') in extreme cases.

If a *yogi* or a *sadhak* indulges in *nirvikalpa samadhi* too frequently or for too long a time at a stretch, and has irregular (as well as unbalanced) dietary habits then there is havoc in the 'Enteric Nervous System'. The gut microbes become restless and under stress, the neurotransmitters that are supposed to be released in the gut (Dopamine – 50% and Serotonin – 90%) are not released properly. Thus, there is total dysbiosis and lack of equilibrium, leading to gut health problems.

To have a life of good health and well-being and to excel in any spiritual *sadhana* at the same time, striking a balance between the two is like tight rope walking and is a 'Self-management Challenge'.

Sri Sri Ramakrishna's stomach disorder was due to poor self-management of his gut and digestive system (the Second Brain) and the *nirvikalpa samadhi* (the First Brain). I don't presume, any Ramakrishna scholar, neither Indian nor foreign has thrown any light on the saint's biology.

Sri Sri Ramakrishna's Brain: Premonition Power

Sri Sri Ramakrishna had a *vision*. Two birds were perching on the branch of a tree. One of them was found to be most restless, while the other was restful, still, calm. Suddenly, Ramakrishna found that the restless bird entered into the restful one and could not be found anywhere anymore. He got the clue that the restless bird *jivatma* merged into the restful one *paramatma*. It was a message for him that time has arrived for him to do *Advaita sadhana*. Within the next few days, naga sannyasi Totapuri came. (Reference 32)

The 'Samadhi Brain State' ('SBS')

A discussion on the 'Samadhi Brain State' ('SBS') that deals with an 'Altered State of Consciousness' ('ASC') can very well begin with a famous Bengali song of Goddess Kali which talks about 'consciousness' as such and '*True Consciousness*'.

'Amar Chetana Chaitanya Kore De Ma Chaitanya Moyee'

(A Very Popular Bengali Goddess Kali's Song Slightly Amended & Translated by the Author into English)

"Oh, My Ever-Conscious Mother! Awaken My Consciousness!
Oh, My Ever-Conscious Mother! Awaken My Consciousness!

I wish to swim into the ocean of your feelings
I wish to swim into the ocean of your feelings!
I wish to cling on to your lotus feet!

Oh, My Ever-Conscious Mother! Awaken My Consciousness!
Please take me out from my own nature of dark ignorance
And put me into your state of mind;
Open up my wisdom eyes
Open up my wisdom eyes
Let me fathom how much wise you are
Do fill in all my voids with the sport of your feelings
All of my this life's bubbling curiosity take into your lotus feet
Allow me to leave my temporary sojourn
By conquering all the Six Enemies of the Mind!

Oh, My Ever-Conscious Mother, Awaken My Consciousness!!
Oh, My Ever-Conscious Mother, Awaken My Consciousness!!

'*Samadhi*' is an altered state of consciousness where the mind is completely absorbed in one object of meditation (Reference 33). In the

'SBS', the soul gets independence from the body and can embark on a journey across the time. This is a very deep state of consciousness in which the brain emits delta brainwaves (0.5–4 hertz or cycles/second).

'*Savikalpa Samadhi*' is when you are focused only on one subject or an object, like the image of a deity. '*Nirvikalpa Samadhi*' is when your mind is blank, you are not focusing on anything. If you remain in that blank state for some time (it depends on practice and varies from person to person), you become exposed to your soul and you get to know your soul closely. *Samadhi* can be with full awareness and consciousness. But it is not always so – there are various stages of *samadhi*, starting with the 'deep sleep' like state of unconscious stone-like (*pashantulya*), and ending with full conscious awareness. After we've reorganised our relationships with the outside world and our own inner world, we come to the finale of bliss.

'*Samadhi*' converts a person to serve humanity selflessly with the knowledge discovered while in the *Samadhi* State. (Reference 34)

The purpose of *Yoga* is to raise the consciousness to higher levels of awareness, culminating in *samadhi*, which is the stage when the self, realising its own true nature, leaves its mortal shell and enters its liberated state.

The practice of *Yoga* starts with *yama* and *niyama* – do's and don'ts in life, renouncing short-term pleasures, which in the language of neuroscience, would be described as 'Dopamine Fasting' ('DF') – control of sensual pleasures. The more we're exposed to the exhilaration of 'Dopamine' ('D'), the more we need to pursue higher levels of stimulation to achieve the same effect. Taking a break from behaviours that trigger strong amounts of 'D' release (especially in repeated fashion) allows our brain to recover and restore itself. Ignoring a stimulus which is likely to release 'D' is an effective way of 'DF'. (Reference 35)

The next step, *asana*, essentially consists of postural and gestural control. Its practice prepares the body to remain in different postures for long periods of time. This step is not essential to be followed by those who have transcended 'body consciousness'. Then comes *pranayama* – for lowering the breath cycle. The next is *pratyahara* – withdrawal of all senses from external engagement. *Pratyahara* is followed by *dharana* – developing inner focus. Next to *dharana* is *dhyana* or 'meditation'. Much though one may succeed to reach up to this stage, effective meditation would not be possible if he cannot perform effective DMN Management – managing the workings of the idle brain. This was a big advantage for Sri Sri Ramakrishna as his DMN was never active – it was totally filled with the thoughts of Goddess Kali. So, he could easily get into '*dhyana*' and then into '*samadhi*'. Some people say that this is the stage when the *kundalini* rises. However, *kundalini* cannot rise unless consciousness is totally withdrawn from the external world. All the nine gates of the body (the mouth, the two eyes, the two ears, the two nostrils, the anus, and the genitals) are totally shut.

During *samadhi*, you discover the real self – the Super Soul. After *samadhi*, the most difficult challenge is to come back to *Sahaj Samadhi* – the world of *Maya*. However, it was not difficult for *Avatar* Sri Sri Ramakrishna.

In the 'SBS', you acquire the knowledge of *brahma* – the cosmic energy. Under such circumstances, brain's rational thinking circuit stops functioning. The person in the 'SBS' becomes speechless; he cannot simply describe what *brahma* is. One who becomes knowledgeable about *brahma*, does not talk to anyone about it. One under the 'SBS' descends again to impart education to the masses.

One brahmin had two sons. He sent both the sons to a *guru* to acquire knowledge about *brahma*. After some time, both the sons returned on completion of their education. The brahmin asked them to tell him what they have learnt about *brahma*. The first son went on reciting from his memory from the *Vedas* and the *Vedanta*. The second son was quiet. He kept silent. The brahmin asked him whether he had learnt anything. This young man said: "*Brahma* is indescribable. It is beyond any description. Once you get the taste of *brahma*, you don't need anything else." (Reference 36)

Time and space would have been transcended in the 'SBS'. After having spent in this state for some time, you see divinity in everything. The intellect goes beyond its normal function of discrimination. The brain's 'Error Detection Circuit' ('EDC') full of 'Error Neurons', becomes dysfunctional. This exulted blissful state may last for a few hours or even a few days. Initially, there is no wish to return from this state and it is said that if one stays at this level for 21 days, there is every possibility that the soul will leave the body for good.

Ramakrishna's *Nirvikalpa Samadhi* Experience at the Instance of Naga Monk Totapuri

After doing the necessary *puja* and providing tips for *sannyas*, Totapuri asked Ramakrishna to get into *nirvikalpa samadhi*. Ramakrishna tried, tried, tried very hard but during his *dhyana* stage he could not free his mind from the thoughts and image of his deity – Goddess Kali. He simply could not make his mind absolutely vacant – free from any thoughts or images. When he couldn't achieve that state of mind after trying hard for three days, he mentioned his problem to Totapuri. Totapuri got very annoyed and said: "I don't understand what is your problem." (He was naturally upset because in his domain, he used to believe and was convinced that God was *nirakar* – devoid of any *rupa* – shape and size.) He found a piece of broken glass on the floor. He took it and pressed it on Ramakrishna's forehead and asked him to concentrate on the wound that had been created. Ramakrishna concentrated his mind by mustering all his willpower and imagined he has a sword at his disposal with which he severed Goddess Kali's image into thin slices and felt that the Goddess's thoughts and image had disappeared totally. He had no other *vikalpa* in his mind and got immersed in deep *samadhi*.

Finding Ramakrishna in *samadhi*, Totapuri sat beside him for a little while then left when he found all the signs of *nirvikalpa samadhi* in his disciple's body. He locked the door of the room where Ramakrishna was in *samadhi* to prevent anyone from disturbing him. He returned to his seat near Panchabati and waited for his disciple to knock on the locked door requesting him to unlock it. One day gone, two days gone, when three days went and there was not a sign of anything from inside, he himself opened the door and found Ramakrishna was sitting just like he had seen him three days ago. He was absolutely inert, totally restful like a dead man.

Totapuri could not believe his eyes. What had taken him forty long years to achieve, his disciple had achieved it in three days. It was really remarkable. Being suspicious, he tried and tested Sri Ramakrishna again and again and was confirmed that it was a fact – his disciple was not feigning anything. He started shouting: "What a *maya* and *leela* of Goddess Kali! It is genuine and authentic *nirvikalpa samadhi*. What I had taken to achieve in forty years, he has done it in three days." He started to take action to take Ramakrishna out from the 'Samadhi Brain State' ('SBS'). (Reference 37)

References

[1] Dilip Kumar Ghosh, *Sri Sri Ramakrishna Punthi: Ek Akshay Shristi* (In Bengali), Kolkata: Sahityasree, 2023, p. 176–177.

[2] Kathleen Davis, "Everything you need to know about DMT", *Medical News Today*, 28th February 2024.

[3] Iris Kulbatski, "Natural High: Endogenous Psychedelics in the Gut and Brain", *TS*, Fall 2023.

[4] 'N, N-Dimethyltryptamine' – *Wikipedia.*

[5] Jose Carlos Bouso *et al.*, "Hallucinations and Hallucinogens: Psychopathology or Wisdom?" *Cult Med Psychiatry*, 2023, Vol. 47, No./Issue 2, pp. 576–604, Published online 12th January 2023.

[6] Jagadish Angadi, "Infusing life into stones" *Deccan Herald*, 17th June 2018.

[7] Adepu Mahender, "Infusing life into stones", *Hans India*, 15th March 2017.

[8] Dilip Kumar Ghosh, *Sri Sri Ramakrishna Punthi: Ek Akshay Shristi* (In Bengali), Kolkata: Sahityasree, 2023, p. 46

[9] Ueli Rutishauser, PhD, "'Error Neurons' Play Role in How Brain Processes Mistakes", *Cedars Sinai*, Los Angeles, 4th December 2018.

[10] Catherine Orr and Robert Hester, "Error-related anterior cingulate cortex activity and the prediction of conscious error awareness", *Frontiers in Human Neuroscience*, 2012, Vol. 6, p.177, Published online 19th June 2012.

[11] N.P. Bechtereva *et al.*, "Error detection mechanism of the brain: background and prospects", *International Journal of Psychophysiology*, Nov-Dec 2005.

[12] Himanshu Joshi, "What is Trigunas? Types (*Sattva, Rajas, Tamas*) of *Trigunas*", Himalayan Yoga Association.

[13] "The Three Temperaments", *tantramag*, 6th January 2016.

[14] "Oxytocin" – *Wikipedia.*

[15] Rajib Sraban, *Jugabatar Sri Sri Ramakrishna: Jana Katha Ajana Bishoy*, (In Bengali) Kolkata: Sen Brothers, 2024, pp. 211–214.

[16] Fr. James McTavish, "Jesus the Divine Physician", *The Linacre Quarterly*, February 2018, Vol. 85, No/Issue 1, pp 18–23. Published online 28th March 2018.

[17] C. Sue Carter *et al.*, "Is Oxytocin 'Nature's Medicine'"? *Pharmacological Reviews,* October 2020, Vol. 72, No./Issue 4, pp. 829–861.

[18] "Altered State of Consciousness" – *Wikipedia.*

[19] Dilip Kumar Ghosh, *Sri Sri Ramakrishna Punthi: Ek Akshay Shristi* (In Bengali), Kolkata: Sahityasree, 2023, p.54.

[20] "Oceanic feeling" – *Wikipedia.*

[21] Siddhartha Ganguli, *SUCCESS: Can Be Planned and Earned*, New Delhi: Allied Publishers, (E-book).

[22] Rajib Sraban, *Jugabatar Sri Sri Ramakrishna: Jana Katha Ajana Bishoy*, (In Bengali), Kolkata: Sen Brothers, 2024, pp. 55–56.

[23] Mihaly Csikszentmihalyi, *Flow: The Psychology of Optimal Experience*, New York: Harper Perennial, 2008.

[24] "Problems in a Householder's Life and Their Solution", Swami Sarvapriyananda Ji, Video Presentation on YouTube, Kathamrita Bhavan, Ramakrishna Math.

[25] Dilip Kumar Ghosh, *Sri Sri Ramakrishna Punthi: Ek Akshay Shristi*, (In Bengali) Kolkata: Sahityasree, 2023, p. 211.

[26] Rajib Sraban, *Jugabatar Sri Sri Ramakrishna: Jana Katha Ajana Bishoy*, (In Bengali); Kolkata: Sen Brothers, 2024, pp. 80–84.

[27] Rajib Sraban, *Jugabatar Sri Sri Ramakrishna: Jana Katha Ajana Bishoy*, (In Bengali), Kolkata: Sen Brothers, 2024, pp. 125–128.

[28] "Human brain" – *Wikipedia.*

[29] "The Gut and the Brain", *Harvard Medical School,* Winter 2017.

[30] Alessandro Silvani *et al.*, "Brain-heart interactions: physiology and clinical applications", *Philosophical Transactions of the Royal Society*, 13th May 2016.

[31] Alanna Cohen, *10% Human: How Your Body's Microbes Hold the Key to Health and Happiness*, London: William Collins, 2015.

[32] Dilip Kumar Ghosh, *Sri Sri Ramakrishna Punthi: Ek Akshay Srishti* (In Bengali), Kolkata: Sahityasree, 2023, p. 100.

[33] "Samadhi" – *Wikipedia*.

[34] "Is it possible to reach Samadhi and never come back to the physical self?" *Quora*.

[35] Whitney Akers, "Is Dopamine Fasting a Way to Fix Your Brain or a Silicon Valley Fad?" *healthline*, 20th November 2019.

[36] Rajib Sraban, *Jugabatar Sri Sri Ramakrishna: Jana Katha, Ajana Bishoy* (In Bengali) Kolkata: Sen Brothers, 2024, p. 195.

[37] Dilip Kumar Ghosh, *Sri Sri Ramakrishna Punthi: Ek Akshay Shristi* (In Bengali), Kolkata: Sahityasree, 2023, p. 104–106.

CHAPTER 3

Sri Sri Ramakrishna's Birth Plan

"When God descends on earth, He comes with two objectives. The first one is: to remove the pollutants from true & pure religion, according to the needs of the time. And, the second one is: to taste the realities. To fulfil these two objectives, He may also bring with Him His most eligible deputies and assistants to earth.

Even if they had been born at different places and at different times in the past, at the appropriate moment, they all meet Him at the same place and, by His grace, get exposed to their real nature and their relationships with Him. This is how they get spiritually groomed to help him, with full heart and soul, in the performance of his twin *sports (leela).* They serve as His different organs and body parts.

As long as God remains in the social life in his *gross body*, they remain and get enjoyment from and with Him and also provide enjoyment to Him. According to His instructions, they chalk out their own spiritual activity plans and implement them. Afterwards, when God leaves His *gross body*, they continue their activities for the welfare & upliftment of the mankind. Once their respective responsibilities are carried out, they also leave their *gross bodies* and become *subtle.*

The above words are very much applicable to Sri Sri Ramakrishna and his apostles. That they were not creatures of this materialistic world, that they had seeds of spirituality in them from their childhood becomes evident when we study their background and history."

—Translated and adapted from the Bengali book
Sri Ramakrishna Bhaktamalika
by Swami Gambhirananda, Kolkata: Udbodhan Karjalay.

[Cross-quoted from Dilip Kumar Ghosh, *Sri Ramakrishner Sri M*, Kolkata: Sahityasree, 2022, p. 26.]

What Was Sri Sri Ramakrishna's Birth Plan

In order to know what Sri Sri Ramakrishna's birth plan was, we have to do an 'ancestral audit' for him. Why is it so, let me explain.

Every living individual is made of four components. The 'body' and the 'brain' are living tissues which are visible and palpable, composed of genes that we inherit from our ancestors – on the father's as well as mother's sides. Then there is the 'mind' which is a collection of neuronal networks that come into existence due to continuous interaction with our living and working environments. 'Mind' is thus an epigenetic product ('epigenetics' is the science of 'genes + environment'). 'Soul' comes from outside. (Reference 1)

As far as the 'brain' is concerned, a child gets its 'forebrain' from its mother. The 'forebrain' is the seat of intelligence and other cognitive powers, the executive control system, and the powers of imagination and visualisation. The 'midbrain' – especially the 'limbic system' (that is, the 'emotional mind') is a gift from the father.

Now, if we take the case of Sri Sri Ramakrishna, we can come to the following conclusions:

1. He had inherited from his mother, her value system [simplicity, humility, egoless-ness (no vanity), faith in divine powers, dispassion towards worldly things like fixed & liquid assets as well as kins and relations – which are all '*mithya*' ('unreal') and '*maya*' ('delusion')] and simple lifestyle.
2. His soul had come from divine sources. Remember his father's dream while he was in Gaya when Lord Vishnu appeared and said that He would be born as Khsudiram's son; and also his mother's experience near her village home when a ray of light came from the nearby Shiva temple and had entered into her lower abdomen following which she became pregnant at an age when women do not bear any child.
3. His parents were not unaccustomed to witness divine visions. In published literature, we find mentions of his father's vision twice or thrice but his mother had experienced visions quite a few times

during her pregnancy and after she had delivered infant Gadai.

4. Since he was a divinely created child, there was no trace of '*kama*' ('lust') in him. '*Kama*' (or 'lust') is the biggest enemy in the spiritual pursuit.
5. '*Tyaga*' or 'renunciation' was inherent in Ramakrishna's nature.

Sri Sri Ramakrishna's birth plan was thus to stand for '*satyam*' and '*satyam*' alone. What is '*satyam*'? We have infatuation for everything that we experience through our senses and which make us 'feel good' leading to the release of the pleasure chemical 'Dopamine' ('D'). All these pleasures are transient, temporary, they do not provide us with sustained happiness and bliss. We eat some good food, we like it, 'D' is released and that 'D' does not remain permanently. It goes away; and we become hungry for another dose of 'D' again. This longing for pleasure – release of 'D' – satisfaction – rise of longing for again – seeking release of 'D' – this cycle is a vicious one – it is '*mithya*' – it is not the truth. The only '*satyam*' is the '*atman*' which is free from any physical longingness as the soul has no sensory organs. When it entered into the Pineal Gland of the foetus's brain at the end of 49 days or 7 weeks of pregnancy it was just a bundle of soul energy. It started operating through the foetus's operating system which had sensory and working organs – not fully developed though.

We are pulled towards '*kam*' ('lust') and '*kanchan*' ('greed') again and again. '*Satyam*' means detachment from, renunciation of these as these are all '*mithya*' ('unreal'/'untruth').

Sri Sri Ramakrishna was unable to touch any metal – including coins, he was so much against all '*mithya*'. Anything man-made is temporary – subject to change. What is true and valuable today becomes false and valueless tomorrow. Paramhansa was a seeker of truth throughout his life.

Longing for '*satyam*' is longing for 'God'. But, how do we access 'God'? First of all, we have to understand the trifling nature of this world. Secondly, we must understand that the only thing that is valuable is 'God' – the 'God' inside us – the 'Soul' – the '*Atman*'. The thoughts of the mind always flow towards what all around us consider valuable. So, the third most important thing is '*satsang*' – to be in noble company – to read books, to watch videos and movies, and to mix with people who have the same 'value system'.

If these three steps are taken, then *vivek* (conscience) would be awakened and *vairagya* (dispassion/disinterest) will come leading us towards the *nitya* (the permanent).

Avatar Sri Sri Ramakrishna was burning purity. One must try to get a slice of his soul to lead a peaceful spiritual life.

Did Sri Sri Ramakrishna Manage Himself According to His Birth Plan

As Gadadhar stepped into his youth, his boyishness disappeared and he became a serious person. At times, he used to think that he has come to this planet to execute some very special responsibility. It was related to reformation, restoration and establishment of sound values. (Reference 3) A spiritual gravity started developing in his personality, although he was a little confused as to what would be his role he would be called upon to play on the stage. He was quite proficient in playing both male and female roles on the village stage but now which and where would be his stage and what all roles he would be required to play?

Sri Sri Ramakrishna's (born on 18th February 1836) birth plan according to Indian astrology (*jyotish shastra*), had been charted out by many, some of which are available on the internet. (Reference 4). His ascendent birth *rashi* was 'Aquarius' (*Kumbha*), but I've my own way of looking at his 'birth plan'.

Gadadhar's (Ramakrishna's boyhood home name) birth was not normal. In the first place, before his birth, his parents experienced some supernatural events. His father Kshudiram Chatterjee had a dream in which Lord Gadadhara (a form of Vishnu) said that he would be born as his son. Chandramani Devi, Gadadhar's mother, is said to have a vision of light entering into her womb from the Shiva Temple (Yogider Shiv Mandir) near her house. So the would-be child had the blessings of both Lord Vishnu (the preserver) and Lord Shiva (of the *shakti* cult). Amazingly, Ramakrishna had a lot of attraction towards the Radha-Krishna *Leela* (as he would often act in the role of the *Gopis* and emulate the different Vaishnava *bhavas*. And, of course, his main attraction was towards Goddess Kali, who in partnership with Lord Shiva, represent the '*shakti* cult'). We don't find much role of Lord Brahma (the creator) in Ramakrishna's life. Although he selected and groomed his apostles, he did not create his own progeny.

The impending descendance of Jesus in the womb of Mary had been experienced by her as a vision. Inside his tomb, on the third day of his burial (known as 'Easter Sunday') Jesus had shared two (2) very deep secrets with His lady devotee, Mary Magdalene. These were: in order to experience God, the seeker must wait to have visions and must hear voices. He had shared these with Mary Magdalane in the form of a vision – in which Mary could SEE him standing in front of her. He was SPEAKING and she was LISTENING. Audition had also featured in the encounter. So, visions and auditions are musts for experiencing true spirituality. (Reference 5). These are the two interfaces by which God has a continuous relationship with the seeker. Ramakrishna had frequent visions and auditions and occasional such experiences by his wife Sarada Devi and his other direct disciples with whom he had shared slices of his soul have also been documented in Ramakrishna literature. The same thing happened with the apostles of Lord Jesus. The whole Book of Revelations is a book of visions.

What Lord Jesus had shared with Mary Magdalane (Reference 6) is that the mind (the 'intellect' – the *buddhi*) is the conduit for spiritual vision which is real 'visualisation' and not 'hallucination'. The mind is positioned between the soul and the spirit. Mind is the higher intellectual faculty comprehending higher truths facilitating the reconciliation between the 'temple' and the 'divine'. ('Where the mind is there is treasure').

How the person who sees the vision – sees it? Through the soul or through the spirit? He sees the vision neither through the soul nor through the spirit, but through the mind, which is the bridge between the two. The mind is often associated with intellect, reason, and higher knowledge. It is the faculty which has the capacity to understand the truth of spiritual visions that those are not hallucinations or daydreaming. It acts as the intermediary between the soul and the divine realm. It is the faculty that comprehends the higher knowledge that is in the vision. The soul is often referred as the psyche which is an intermediate aspect of human consciousness. It is the seat of emotions, desires, and individuality (that is, ego). Soul is on a journey of spiritual ascent seeking to transcend the material world and unite with the divine (in Hinduism, the *Jivatma* wanting to merge with the *Paramatma*). The soul may have experiences of vision guided by the higher knowledge. The spirit is the innermost aspect of the human being (that is, *prana* in Hinduism). It is the divine spark or essence within each individual that is connected to the ultimate source of divinity. The spirit seeks to return to its divine origin and the mind and the soul play roles to facilitate this return. The mind comprehends the spiritual vision. It acts as the intermediary that allows the soul to access higher knowledge and insight. A properly cultivated mind is a higher intellectual faculty that helps the individual to understand and interpret spiritual experiences. (Reference 7)

That is why the mind is often the first target of evil forces like the 'Six Enemies of the Mind'. Ramakrishna had a mind which was free from these 'Six Enemies' and he was most vigilant not to be affected by any contamination, using self-management strategies like sudden 'fainting' and '*bhav samadhi*'.

Avatar Ramakrishna's birth plan was to combine *prema* ('*bhakti*' in the Vaishnava sense) with *shakti* spiritual power) to purify himself by getting trained in and tasting different religions and share slices of his soul with most eligible people, especially youngsters, who will pursue his philosophy and carry on his mission. And, he could achieve it amazingly well before he left this planet.

Sri Sri Ramakrishna's Vision

"Christ has no body now but yours. No hands, no feet on earth but yours. Yours are the eyes through which he looks compassion on this world. Yours are the feet with which he walks to do good. Yours are the hands through which he blesses all the world. Yours are the hands, yours are the feet, yours are the eyes, you are his body. Christ has no body now on earth but yours. (Goodreads)

Teresa of Avila

Teresa of Avila, also called Saint Teresa of Jesus, was a Carmelite nun and prominent Spanish mystic and religious reformer. Active during the Counter-Reformation, Teresa became the central figure of a movement of spiritual and monastic renewal, reforming the Carmelite Orders of both men and women. Her autobiography, *The Life of Teresa of Jesus,* and her books, *The Interior Castle* and *The Way of Perfection* are prominent works on Christian mysticism and Christian meditation practice. (Reference 8)

Echoing with Teresa of Avila, I can speculate what Sri Sri Ramakrishna used to visualise regarding his relationship with Goddess Kali:

"I, Gadadhar, has no body now but yours, my Mother! No hands, no feet on earth but yours. Yours are the eyes through which I look compassionately on this world. Yours are the feet with which I walk to do good. Yours are the hands through which I bless all the world. Yours are the hands, yours are the feet, yours are the eyes, you are my body. I, Gadadhar, have no body now on earth but yours!"

This thought, continuously muttered as 'self-talk' would allow Sri Sri Ramakrishna's soul to merge with the divine soul during his *nirvikalpa samadhi* (ultimate enlightenment). (Reference 9) Since he practised it regularly, he had developed the skill of getting on and off the *samadhi* state at will. When Totapuri Baba (References 10, 11 & 12) came to train him in the philosophy of advaita and a few critical spiritual techniques, he was utterly surprised to find how much advanced was Sri Sri Ramakrishna in attaining *nirvikalpa samadhi.*

Madman Has Descended to Cure Madness

A man who has come to this world to cure madness, how can he himself be mad? Sarada Devi thought. She had come to meet her husband at his Kamarpukur house after a gap of a few years. She had heard from all around that her husband had turned totally mad.

She had a conviction that he is not properly understood by one who meets him once or twice only – casually, formally. She had heard many stories from people who had seen how her husband conducted himself in Dakhshineswar. Some of them heard him singing a devotional song, some others found him dancing like Lord Shiva, some others saw him prostrating and rolling on the floor like a Sufi mystic and a devotee of Islam, some saw him dressed like Sri Radhika mad to get close to Lord Krishna, some others found him jumping like a monkey – when he was playing the role of Lord Hanuman; a few others observed him in the *samadhi* state. 'Money' was of no value to Gadadhar, he used to equate it with ordinary soil; although the whole human society was running on 'money'. According to him women were not machines for reproduction which men can use for their carnal pleasure. Women were mothers – they were creators and groomers; they were care-givers. He was very much against creating offsprings as he knew that most children were children of lust, and not of love. (Reference 14). Thakur Ramakrishna and Ma Sarada's role were not to become biological parents; they were meant to be parents to the whole world – that is what they have been ever since their divine existence was recognised. (Reference 13)

She believed that these were not signs of any madness; these were the sports (*leela*) of a specially empowered person who has been brought in the mortal form for an altogether different purpose. He had descended on earth to establish, in his own ingenious simple way, that there was no difference between the 'key' religions. The message was the same: shed your ego, love everything and everyone, find the presence of God in everything and everyone.

Sarada Devi was a little more advanced than Thakur in removing the caste barrier from her value system. While at Kamarpukur in her husband's village, she had cleaned up the place where Srinivas, a low caste person, close to Gadadhar (his boyhood playmate) had his mid-day meal as an invitee to Gadai's house. This act of hers was not regarded as fair by the villagers. They had a value system where the landlord (*zamindar*) had the highest status in the society. Next in the hierarchy came the brahmins who used to perform the worshipping and religious duties related to the gods and goddesses, provide counsel and advice to others whenever they sought, read and taught *shastras*, eat well and leave well, which did not have any physical toiling included. All the toiling, hard and manual work had to be done by people who belonged to lower castes. The lower caste people were supposed to serve the brahmins and landlords. In the backdrop of such a culture and value system, what Sarada had done had just not been found acceptable to the Kamarpukur villagers. Sarada Devi was the first to break this custom which had her husband's total approval. She did it with the spirit of love, judging Srinivas not by his caste but by his being a human. She did it with all fairness to him as a guest who is equivalent to God. She displayed true spirituality.

Everyone is human – there is no community and caste difference. Community and caste are all man-made. Everyone deserves to be treated with equal love and respect. Otherwise, you're practicing aspirituality. (Reference 15)

A Different Route Altogether

Sri Sri Ramakrishna, according to his birth plan, followed a totally different route altogether. It was just the opposite of the path followed by the members of the society in his days. He journeyed along the path of restraint, renunciation, self-control and total indifference to worldly things which common people long for. His longing was only for the Truth. To achieve that end, he had made himself an instrument in the hands of the Goddess. As he evolved into the REAL RAMAKRISHNA, he stayed most comfortably and conveniently in one place to lead the then society to a different spiritual domain.

When he gained knowledge about REALITY and put it in his storehouse, many people started visiting him from many places – some of which were far-flung, located in deep interiors. Being exposed to his divine vision and truth, they not only became blessed but also started sharing with others wherever they went.

Sri Sri Ramakrishna's sport (*leela*) with his devotees was to spread his generous thoughts. But the special feature was that all his close associates who later became his apostles were much younger than him in age. And, some of them were more educated (but not more enlightened) than him. He, nevertheless, didn't got much time to educate and transform his devotees. His way of transforming young devotees were, as I've already discussed: by sharing a slice of his soul; by touching them with his hands or foot; by sharing eye contact, smile and sweet words impregnated with divine magnetism. (Reference 16)

Let me share a wonderful example of Thakur's special strategy for sharing a slice of his soul. Thakur, with his ailing health, was staying in the house of Balaram Basu in North Calcutta. There he had shared a slice of his soul with a brahmin who was a devotee of Sri Gouranga. When that brahmin came to pay his respect to him, finding him dressed like a Vaishnava, he greeted him with folded hands. Paramhansa was fanning himself with a hand fan. The young brahmin was wondering in his mind how he can get an opportunity to serve Thakur so that his life became blessed. The all-knowing Paramhansa could read the young brahmin's mind and most happily he handed over the hand fan to him. The brahmin was only too happy to be of service to the avatar. Thakur was very happy with his spirit of service – he went into a *bhava* and kept a foot on the chest of the brahmin as if he was Goddess Kali (he had the skill to invoke the Goddess's spirit in him) and the brahmin was Lord Shiva who had the attitude of total surrender. The brahmin could feel the ecstasy of the experience. The name of the young brahmin was Nrityagopal Goswami.

Swami Saradananda wrote: "I entered into the house somehow and saw that on the western side of the room, facing the East, Thakur was in a *samadhi* state. His face was beaming with a smile representing a feeling of genuine happiness. His right foot was raised and put forward. A man sitting in front of him had placed Thakur's foot on his chest with great love and adoration. The man who was sitting like that, his eyes were shut and his face and chest were getting drenched with tears flowing from his eyes. The house was absolutely quiet and the vibrations that one could feel there were absolutely divine. (Reference 17)

Sri Sri Ramakrishna made his close associates imbibe deep insights, and he prepared them to propagate his typical message of 'There are as many routes as there are schools of thought' (In Bengali: '*Jato Mat Tato Path*'). He really did a lot in too short a time. Even now, being unseen and invisible, he is getting work done by his devotees and others convinced about his philosophy, to establish peace and harmony in the world and to free people from their chronic bickering and frustrations.

Spreading Positive Vibes

Avatar Sri Sri Ramakrishna was born to spread positive vibes. Once Gadadhar had come to spend some time in his village Kamarpukur and from there he had gone to his sister's home in the Sihor village. His sister was Gadadhar's constant companion Hriday's mother. Hriday's younger brother Rajaram had taken him to a nearby village pond. He was sitting there near the steps close to the water. After a little while, a school of fishes of different shapes and sizes assembled close to him, as if they could feel his positive vibes. He started playing with them. They also played with him merrily.

Just when he thought that he will call Rajaram and would leave the place, a large-sized fish jumped out of water and landed near his feet. He took it up fondly and let it go back into the water.

Rajaram was watching everything from a distance and he was wondering: "Oh My God! Is this possible? I've heard from others that my cousin was quite different from other people in general. Now I find, whatever I'd heard about him is all true. He seems to have a divine streak in him which releases positive vibes otherwise why the fishes, instead of running away from him, would move closely to him and start playing merrily?" (Reference 18)

Lead Life According to Your Birth Plan

Sri Sri Ramakrishna's nephew and constant companion Hriday had a sudden plan to lead his life like his uncle Gadadhar. He had lost his wife of late and wanted to become a *sadhak*. He would notice that, from time to time, Gadadhar used to disappear in the garden at the back of the temple, especially at nights. One day he followed him and was amazed to see his uncle – not as a human of flesh-blood-bones-and-tendons but as a glowing ball of light. His body glow had made the moonlight pale. And, he was not walking with his feet on the ground; he was erect but moving forward by floating in the air, his feet not touching the ground. Hriday imagined light coming out of his body also and that he was also not his usual self.

He shouted: "Uncle! We are not ordinary men – you and I. We have come to serve some special purpose. What are we doing here in Dakshineswar? Let us go from place to place. We have to lead people to spirituality."

Ramakrishna heard Hriday and came to him. He said: "Don't shout. Be cool!" Hriday went on speaking like mad. Gadadhar quickly touched his chest and said: "Mother Goddess! Make him an inert lifeless being!" The moment he touched Hriday, Hriday's enthusiasm vanished. He touched his uncle's feet and started crying: "What have you done? Why did you spoil my mood? I was so happy, so much carried away. You spoilt everything."

Ramakrishna commented: "You were being too ambitious. Your time and turn have not come yet. When your time and turn will come, you'll experience everything."

Hriday disappeared. After a little while, Ramakrishna heard his scream: "My body is burning. Please save me. I had sat here to do some meditation but somebody has put burning charcoal on my body!!"

Ramakrishna sat by his side and started caressing him. Then he said: "I'd told you that you'll get everything when your time and turn will come. Move according to your birth plan. If you want to deviate from the plan, it will never work out; instead, there will be disaster. Time is not yet ripe for you." As Ramakrishna touched Hriday's body with great affection and love, he was totally transformed. He promised that he will remain the same Hriday and wouldn't aspire to be like his uncle Ramakrishna. (Reference 19)

References

[1] Siddhartha Ganguli, *Goddess Kali, God Thoughts, Sri Sri Ramakrishna and A Few Slices of Sri Sri Ramakrishna's Soul (Introducing 'SoulOlogy')*, Noida: Allied Publishers Pvt. Ltd., 2024.

[2] "Sri Ramakrishna and Longing for God" video presentation on YouTube by Swami Shuddidananda, Advaita Ashram, Talk delivered in R K Mission, Delhi on 9th April 2023.

[3] Rajib Sraban, *Jugabatar Sri Sri Ramakrishna: Jana Katha Ajana Bishoy*, (In Bengali) Kolkata: Sen Brothers, 2024, p. 45.

[4] "Thorough Analysis of Ramakrishna Paramhansa Chart" – Sheevi Caroline.

[5] "The Two Secrets Jesus Revealed to ONLY Mary Magdalene" – Quoracles Digital Gospel, Video on YouTube.

[6] "Two Secrets Jesus Revealed to ONLY Mary Magdalane – How the 12 Disciples Reacted" Epic History Explorers, Video on YouTube.

[7] "The 2 Secrets Jesus Shared with Mary Magdalene" Bible Stories, Video on YouTube.

[8] "Teresa of Avila" – *Wikipedia.*

[9] Dumuzzi, 'Nirvikalpa Samadhi and what it is like to exist in a non-dual state' *r/hinduism.*

[10] "Totapuri Baba" *Secrets of the Siddhas – Health, Longevity and Enlightenment*, 15th April 2021.

[11] "Ramakrishnaji Meets Totapuri", Video Presentation on YouTube by 'ausarmaat'.

[12] "Totapuri Baba", Video Presentation on YouTube by 'Ashrams of India'.

[13] Rajib Sraban, *Jugabatar Sri Sri Ramakrishna: Jana Katha, Ajana Bishoy*, (In Bengali), Kolkata: Sen Brothers, 2024, pp. 85–88.

[14] Siddhartha Ganguli: *Love: A Good Medicine (The Saga of the Elixir of Life) (Introducing 'LoveOlogy')*, Noida, Allied Publishers Pvt. Ltd., 2023.

[15] Rajib Sraban, *Jugabatar Sri Sri Ramakrishna: Jana Katha, Ajana Bishoy*, (In Bengali), Kolkata: Sen Brothers, 2024, pp. 89–92.

[16] Dilip Kumar Ghosh, *Sri Sri Ramakrishna Punthi: Ek Akshay Srishti* (In Bengali), Kolkata: Sahityasree, 2023, pp. 185–186.

[17] Dilip Kumar Ghosh, *Sri Sri Ramakrishna Punthi: Ek Akshay Srishti* (In Bengali), Kolkata: Sahityasree, 2023, pp. 209–210.

[18] Rajib Sraban, *Jugabatar Sri Sri Ramakrishna: Jana Katha Ajana Bishoy* (In Bengali), Kolkata: Sen Brothers, 2024, p. 162.

[19] Rajib Sraban, *Jugabatar Sri Sri Ramakrishna: Jana Katha Ajana Bishoy*, Kolkata: Sen Brothers, 2024, pp. 154–155.

CHAPTER 4

The 'Real' Ramakrishna

Sri Sri Ramakrishna's REAL Love for Goddess Kali

That Sri Sri Ramakrishna had REAL Love for Goddess Kali is very well-expressed in this song:

"Mother! May my tears fall in torrents only in front of you
Mother! May my tears fall in torrents only in front of you
For no one else, nowhere else, not a single drop shall fall.

Mother! May my tears fall in torrents only in front of you.
You are closer to me than my own self, the queen of my heart
May I know and understand, Mother, that you are the guide across the ocean of existence.

Mother! May my tears fall in torrents only in front of you.
You are infinite, you are indivisible,
Mother, you reside in the inner sanctum.
You are the truth, you are eternal, may this be my constant understanding.

Mother! May my tears fall in torrents only in front of you.
For no one else, nowhere else, not a single drop shall fall."
(Reference 1)

Goddess Kali's Power Working Through Her Child Sri Sri Ramakrishna

The aged Hindu monk Totapuri was a staunch believer in formless ('*nirakar*') God. He did not agree with Sri Sri Ramakrishna that God can have a form ('*sakar*'). After he had completed his initiation of the Paramhansa in the Advaita school of Hinduism, he did not leave Dakhshineswar; he continued to stay, such was the spell of the Paramhansa who was so much full of simplicity and humility.

Nevertheless, these two *sadhaks* used to have their disagreements and conflicts quite often. On some days, if Ramakrishna had skipped his meditation schedule, Totapuri would immediately point out and say: "Unless you meditate and do your *dhyana* regularly, you will be out of practice and it would be difficult for you to concentrate when you try to meditate even after a short gap. Take the case of a brass or a copper pot. Unless you clean it properly regularly, it will collect dust and would not be shining bright. Regular meditative practice will keep your mind clean and pure." Totapuri Ji did not know that Ramakrishna's mind was so much filled to the brim with the thoughts of Mother Goddess Kali that there was no scope for his mind becoming polluted and contaminated with any other thoughts. Totapuri, being a very senior *sadhak* was much better than normal or ordinary; but *avatar* Ramakrishna was supernormal, extraordinary – he had descended on the earth to provide the right guidance, the right direction to those who needed.

Ramakrishna had asked Totapuri once: "Sadhu Baba, you have already attained *siddhi,* still why do you follow the rituals so meticulously every day?" Totapuri showed him the few puja accessories he had, made of metal, and said: "Just like these have to be cleaned regularly, similarly our mind needs regular cleansing." This was a regular issue that came up during the interaction of the two.

As a matter of fact, Ramakrishna was in *bhaktimarg,* whereas Totapuri was in *advaitamarg. Bhaktimarg* is where you have dedicated yourself totally, surrendered your gross and subtle bodies to the deity of your devotion ('*bhakti*'). Totapuri thought *bhaktimarg* was a most peculiar and weird concept. One evening, Ramakrishna was clapping and singing a *kirtan* ('*nam sankirtan*' is chanting of the name of the God or Goddess to whom you're devoted). Totapuri had never seen such an activity in his *advaita* practices. He took it most lightly and was curious to know why Ramakrishna was using hand gestures as if he was making a *roti.* Being from Punjab, Totapuri was familiar with *rotis* very well.

Observing such a predominant gap in the understanding between the two *sadhus*, the more intelligent one amongst the two, Sri Sri Ramakrishna, decided – secretly, in his mind, that he will teach Totapuri about the powers of spirituality based on divine energies having specific forms of gods and goddesses. His Mother Goddess Kali was the one ready at hand. He planned to take Her help.

What a strange coincidence!! This must have been the Goddess's plan. Within the next 2–3 days, after this incident, Totapuri suddenly got afflicted with stomach problem. He had blood dysentery. He started suffering from acute stomach pain which was so severe that he had to roll his body on the ground to get some relief.

One night, his stomach pain was so bad that he wanted to put an end to his life by drowning in deep Ganges water. He proceeded towards the holy river. Got into the shallow water near the bank – started walking towards the middle of the river but, strangely enough, the depth of water did not change – it remained shallow throughout; the deeper zone couldn't be accessed. He reached almost the middle of the river but the water was mid-body deep still.

Most frustrated, he broke down with tears and came running to Ramakrishna and exclaimed: "I do not know what is happening to me!" He narrated his entire experience to Paramhansa. He appealed to Ramakrishna and begged him to get a remedy to his severe stomach ache. Ramakrishna smiled and suggested: "Go to the temple and share your problem with Goddess Kali there. You ought to get a solution." Totapuri did exactly as Ramakrishna had told him. After he poured out his mind to the Goddess, he found all his pains and aches had disappeared. This very incident helped him do develop FAITH in divinity with form ('*sakar*' *adhytmabad*). He slept well, most peacefully, after so many nights.

The next morning, Ramakrishna went to meet Totapuri and asked him how he was feeling. He found Totapuri in an unusually happy mood. He said that his illness had vanished most miraculously. He said my illness had served me as my path-finder. He said that he had received the blessings of Goddess Kali on the previous night.

Both of them went to the temple together and sat down in front of the Goddess to express their deep gratitude. After a few days, totally charged with new vigour, Totapuri left Dakshineswar for good.

This is a very good example of how the *shakti* of Goddess Kali worked through her child – Ramakrishna Paramhansa. This *shakti* works on the subtle body ('*sukshma sarira*') which, in turn, brings about a positive change on the gross body ('*sthula sarira*'). (Reference 2)

Faith Makes Impossible Possible

In Hindu *puranas*, we find the story of an *asura* king Hiranyakashipu. He and his army used to remain engaged in battle most of the time. Once, when a fierce battle was on, the king's pregnant wife had taken shelter in the *ashram* of Narada Muni. Narada Muni used to chant the name of Lord Vishnu several times in a day and the chants used to enter the ears of the foetus and get impregnated into its brain. The child Prahlada when born, he became a devotee of Lord Vishnu right from his birth. The father Hiranyakashipu never believed in any god or goddess as he was a demon. When Prahlada grew up a little, the king asked him: "Son! You believe in your God Hari! And, you also believe that he is everywhere. Do you think he is also inside the pillar of the palace?" Young Prahlada said: "Yes! Of course, Father! He is everywhere." The king asked him for the second time and the answer was the same. Finally, Lord Vishnu (Hari) came out from the pillar of the palace; so strong was the faith of the prince. He had faced a lot of problems in his life, but every time Lord Vishnu saved him. (Reference 3)

On this very topic, Ramakrishna had once narrated the story of a milkmaid who owned cows and used to stay in a remote village. Every morning, she will milk her cows and sell the milk to earn her livelihood. This woman had a guru whose ashram was located some distance away from the milkmaid's village. However, every morning she had to take some milk to the *ashram* to be consumed by the ashramites. Since she had to cross a river on the way, sometimes she will be late to reach the *ashram* as there was only one boat available to cross the river and the boatman might have already taken a passenger who came before her. She had to wait until the boat came back to take her. The *guru* was annoyed with her for her periodic delays and he wanted an explanation. When the milkmaid gave him the reason for her delays, he said: "Oh, is it so? You can't solve this problem? Have faith on God, take his name and He will take you across the river without the boatman's assistance." She had firm belief in God and also on her *guru*; so, she tried it next time when the boat was not available. And, without any hassle, she could cross the river on foot even with the milk-pot in her hand.

Now that she was coming on time, the *guru* became curious to know how she could make it. She told him straight that she had been following his tips. Being suspicious, the *guru* accompanied her to the river. As the boat was not available, the milkmaid walked across merrily but the *guru* got stuck as his mind got diverted as his clothes were getting wet. He became busy in managing his clothes. He was left behind. (Reference 4)

So, the lesson is: if you've firm faith and mind totally focused on the task, you can make even impossibles possible.

There is an episode in the original myth of 'The Exodus' in the Hebrew Bible on the Crossing of the Red Sea or Parting of the Red Sea. It tells us of the escape of the Israelites, led by Moses, from the pursuing Egyptians. Moses holds out his staff and God parts the waters of the Red Sea. With the water dispersed, the Israelites were able to walk on dry ground and cross the sea, followed by the Egyptian army. Once the Israelites had safely crossed, Moses drops his staff, closing the sea, and drowning the pursuing Egyptians. (References 5, 6 & 7)

I'll share an example from Sri Sri Ramakrishna's own life as an example of: how faith heals. When Sri Sri Ramakrishna was suffering too much from pain in his throat, his great devotee playwright Girish Chandra Ghosh landed one day, unannounced, at the Dakshineswar temple. He was coaxing and cajoling Thakur to have something solid like rice to eat. Thakur was not able to eat anything solid for the last few days. Thakur said to Girish: "How can I consume rice? I can't have anything liquid even going down my throat. Drinking something liquid is also so painful."

Girish Ghosh had very high respect for Ramakrishna. So, he said: "I know somebody who is very powerful. I'd request him to share some of his power with me and I will blow air through my mouth on your throat and the pain will disappear." Girish actually thought of none other than Sri Ramakrishna and prayed to him mentally. Then, he blew air on Thakur's throat through his mouth three times. Sri Ramakrishna touched his throat with his own fingers and said: "What a wonder! The pain has disappeared altogether!" (Reference 8)

How Previous Births' Good Deeds Give You Handsome Dividend in the Present Birth

One Tantrik was performing *sadhana* on a human corpse, near a cremation ground, deep inside a dense forest. He was worshipping the Supreme Goddess. His mind was so disturbed that he could not concentrate on his meditation. This restless *sadhak* was attacked by a tiger. He was killed and taken away by the ferocious beast. The human corpse and all his *puja* arrangements and accessories were left intact.

A wood-cutter was felling a big tree in a nearby area. Since it was dark, he couldn't return to his village as it would have been too risky to walk back to his home which was some distance away. This man had climbed up a tree, and he watched how the tiger attacked the *sadhak*, killed him and took him away.

After a little while he came down from the tree, rode on the human corpse and started performing his worship by chanting *mantras.* He didn't have to wait for long and was taken by surprise that the Goddess had appeared before him. The Goddess had a happy face; she seemed to be quite pleased. She told the wood-cutter: "I'm very happy with you. You can stop your *puja* now and ask for my blessings and boon." Her statement was taken as a total surprise by the wood-cutter who asked her: "Mother Goddess! I don't understand one thing. The Tantrik *sadhak* was worshipping you with full devotion; there was nothing lacking in the arrangements that he had made. But still, why did you not protect him? And I've not even progressed a little in my *puja*, you stopped me and you say you're very happy with me – so much so you are ready to offer me your precious blessings and also grant my wish – whatever I want. Would you please explain to me?"

The Goddess smiled and said, my satisfaction is not based on only one life's performance. I take a decision, as to whether I will reward or punish somebody, is based on your previous lives' performances. In the *Tantrik sadhak's* 'balance sheet' there is no profit that has accrued from his past lives' good deeds. Besides, there is another solid reason why he was not rewarded. Whereas, if I examine your previous lives' performances, you have been most anxiously longing for me in your past few lives; you never gave up; you waited most patiently. So, in your 'profit & loss account', there is profit accrual. So, you are eligible for a reward."

"Another very important point. Different people are pulled by different strings. One who is obsessed about fixed and liquid assets, wealth and prosperity, he is pulled by the wealth string. One who obsessed about his family – spouse and kids, he/she is pulled by the family string. One who is obsessed about prestige, status and authority, he is pulled by the status string. In order for the Goddess to appear before you, you have to a pull which is the sum total of all the three. I've found it existent in your case, so I've appeared to bless you." The wood-cutter was overwhelmed.

We want to get blessings from God not by severing any of the strings that I've mentioned, but by forsaking the causes of those obsessions and pulls, by adding all their strong forces together. Naturally, although we perform *pujas* and celebrate festivals with big fanfare, we don't get any blessing from the God, instead we may be punished. (Reference 9)

Sri Sri Ramakrishna as a REAL Husband

Most husbands use their wives as bundles of flesh. I know of an army sepoy who used to keep his rifle under the bed. He would show it to his wife to threaten her if she was reluctant to allow her body for his sexual entertainment. Have you ever noticed that animals and birds have procreational sex only? During their mating season, they go for frequent sexual intercourse because of the high mortality rate of their offsprings. Those who go for recreational sex or sex for entertainment, their purpose is to earn their molecules of Dopamine (D), (References 10 & 11) for them the *shastras* have not kept any provision of classification of men, according to which there are people having: *poshu bhava* (pre-human), *naro* or *veera bhava* (human) and *divya bhava* (post-human). (Reference 12) Men who enjoy the flesh of women, they are even beneath or below the *poshu* or animalish category. (Is that the reason why *aghoris* and *kapaliks* go for consumption of human flesh and intercourse with female corpses?) (Reference 13)

Sri Sri Ramakrishna never looked at his wife Ma Sarada as an object for enjoyment, recreation, or entertainment. He had a very high level of spiritual intelligence (Reference 14) which could make him realise with conviction that even if he and Ma Sarada had created a child, it would not have possessed the qualities they would be looking for in their offspring. He was aware of the famous puranic tale of the king of monsters or demons Hiranyakashipu whose only son Prahlada was just the opposite – anti-demonic, a devotee of Lord Vishnu right from his foetal stage. (Reference 15) So, when Sarada, most tactfully, wanted to know whether she will ever be a mother, Thakur said: "Of course, you will be the mother of many children, you will see." The devotees of Mother Goddess Kali are united in one respect – they are all devoted to the Goddess. 'Devotion' is the link between them. Ramakrishna, who had done *Soroshi Puja* when Sarada was seventeen or eighteen would possibly look at her as a goddess, a replica of Ma Kali and all her devotees' and disciples' minds will have a common link – devotion for Ma Sarada. What a level of spiritual intelligence!!

Many husbands in our culture earn Dopamine by criticising their wives, commanding their wives, and inflicting their Big Egos on their wives. Sri Sri Ramakrishna was just the opposite – an embodiment of humility. Just one striking example will clear confusion, if you have any. Once Ramakrishna was lying on bed in his room with his face looking away from the entrance door to the room. He could hear the sound of the door opening and someone entering into the room. Since the person who entered did not utter any words or make any sound, Thakur had only guessed that it must have been his niece Lakhsmi.

So, he said in a little commanding voice: "Shut the door while going" (In Bengali: "*Jabar samay darja ta lagiye jas!*" (In Bengali '*tui*' – '*tokari*' terms are used between intimate friends and senior-to-junior conversations.) Then, when he suddenly turned around and found Ma Sarada Devi instead, he was so embarrassed that he took out his tongue like Goddess Kali (who had become embarrassed to find Lord Shiva slipped his body underneath his foot to control her fierce thirst for killing people and drinking their blood – Ramakrishna was really Kali's child). (Reference 16). Later on, on several occasions he had requested his niece Lakhsmi to enquire with Sarada whether she was annoyed with him as he had used not a befitting polite language. He had also asked Sarada directly if she had minded and got the response that she didn't attach any importance to it, she was so much devoted to him. Her brain's 'Error Detection Circuit' ('EDC') used to be totally inactive while in Thakur's company – even when thinking about him and his behaviour. (Reference 17)

During the *Shoroshi Puja*, Ramakrishna had given a bath to Ma Sarada, dressed her in a special sari and decked her up in golden ornaments (Mathur Babu had purchased a lot of gold ornaments to be used by Ramakrishna during his *madhura bhava* when he used to feel and behave like a female – as if he was Sri Radhika who was all decked up to entice Lord Krishna Bhagawan.) On other special festive occasions also Ramakrishna used to dress up Ma Sarada in special saris and jewellery so that she looked like a goddess herself. (Reference 18)

In the householder society, many husbands burst out at their wives when the wives take a long time to dress up in gorgeous saris and expensive ornaments. The husband says: "Why do you have to spend so much time in dressing up and decorating yourself – you are already married, and I do not indulge in any infidel behaviour? Are you looking for another man because you're not happy with me, or would you like people to look at you as a goddess instead of looking at the goddess in the pandal who is being worshipped?" A middle-aged husband may say: "You already look old. Your make-up and deck-up – do you think will make you look young and you'll get a suitor younger than me for the rest of your life?" (This kind of message represents the animal instinct as we find an older bitch goes for a younger dog and wants have puppies with it.)

Sri Sri Ramakrishna as a REAL Son

Sri Sri Ramakrishna was Kali's Child – Her REAL son. Although he had his biological mother Chandra Devi for whom he had heart full of love and tremendous respect (as she was the parent who practically brought him up after the sudden demise of his father Khsudiram when he was very young), he was closer, more playful and open with the Goddess. He used to say quite often that he would talk to Her, play with Her, cry to Her for her company just like a kitten mews for the mother cat. In fact, as a young boy in his Kamarpukur village home, he used to sculpt images of Goddess Kali, so skilfully that those images that looked alive. Later on, as a dividend from Thakur's painstaking *sadhana*, he could invoke Ma Kali's soul into his own personality. Once, when he was very indisposed and ill, he had asked his disciples to make all arrangements for Kali Puja. All arrangements were made, but everybody wondered as to what will be worshipped as there was neither any image nor any pot to represent the image. They were hesitant to ask Thakur and were all amazed when he started worshipping himself and everyone genuinely felt that Goddess Kali's spirit had descended into him. (References 19 & 20)

Apart from Chandra Devi, another elderly woman from the neighbourhood, Dhani Kamarni, was very close to Gadadhar. In fact, she was very much present when a ray of radiant light entered into the lower abdomen of Gadai's mother when they were chatting near the local Shiva temple. Dhani was a witness to this event. Some Ramakrishna scholars claim that Dhani played a very important role in Gadadhar's childhood and boyhood sport (*leela*). Dhani was not only present with Chandra when Gadai was born but she also used to extend a helping hand whenever Chandra needed when she was bringing up the child.

Dhani Kamarni was from a low caste, being from the family of blacksmiths. But she had confided in young Gadadhar that she would like to give alms to him and feed him first at the time of his sacred thread. Gadai was so much full of love and compassion for her that he had promised to her that it will be done. When the time came, Gadadhar expressed to his elder brother Ram Kumar, who was making all arrangements for the thread ceremony, that he would like Dhani Kamarni to be the first to give her alms. There were objections from all around on the ground of caste but since Gadai was most insistent, everybody had to agree. So, one can see what was the perception of Gadadhar about who could be the REAL mother. REAL motherhood is not on the basis of biology, religion, caste or creed – it is on the basis of the level of 'Oxytocin' in your blood that you have in the company of a particular lady. It can be measured clinically – but it can also be felt when you feel that you can safely trust that woman – she will never ditch you. (References 21 & 22)

Debendranath Bandyopadhyay was a staunch devotee of Sri Sri Ramakrishna. He had once come to Thakur with his wife and elderly mother. Debendranath's mother had brought some local sweets to be offered to the Goddess in the temple. She had kept those in a special cloth packet. For Ramakrishna, Debendra had brought some expensive sweets. They came by boat and when they reached Dakshineswar it was in the afternoon and too hot. Thakur was seated on his cot in his room. Everyone started offering respectful greeting to Thakur, but Debendra's mother was like a statue. By looking at Ramakrishna, she had motherly feeling ('*vatsalya bhav*'). Ramakrishna could realise her feeling instantly. He got up from his bed, held the old lady by her hand and helped her to sit on his cot. He treated her like his own mother and began talking to her asking more about herself just like a son talks to his mother when he meets her after a break. Ramakrishna told the lady that he would like to have the local sweets which Debendra's mother had with her in a cloth bag. He was keen to have those sweets which the lady had brought although there were many other types of more delicious sweets. The old lady had forgotten that she had brought those local sweets to be offered to the goddess. Debendra didn't know about it; so, he sent somebody out to get such local sweets. Meanwhile, Ramakrishna started pulling the old lady's sari and the cloth bag containing the local sweets fell on the floor. Thakur opened the cloth bag and was exhilarated to find what he had been looking for – the village sweets made from jaggery. He started eating those and one could see how happy he was from his expressions. He used to have similar ecstasy when he used to eat from the *bhog* offered to the goddess.

On another occasion, Sri Sri Ramakrishna had invited the old mother of Manmohan Mitra for lunch at the temple. Manmohan had brought his mother and his son and daughter and Thakur was very pleased. He was overwhelmed with happiness. Thakur had made the guest sit for lunch; he sat a little away from them. Suddenly, what occurred in his mind, nobody knows. He put a full fish-head on a dish and gave it to Manmohan's mother. And the old lady ate up the whole fish-head without any hesitation. In those days, Hindu widows were supposed to have only vegetarian food. On returning home, Manmohan asked his mother what made her break the rule. The old lady said: "That was Thakur's prasad and prasad is not considered as anything eatable as food." It was a gesture of love and compassion of a son for his mother. (Reference 23)

Sri Sri Ramakrishna's REAL Marriage

Are marriages planned and made in heaven? Rarely so. Most love marriages are products of transient infatuation. Arranged marriages are usually fixed by matching the horoscopes of the bride and the bridegroom. Now, astrology certainly is a science based on *astronomy* but how many astrologers today are thoroughly knowledgeable on the subject. Most of them start their practice with little learning. Even if some of them are knowledgeable, can they prevent whatever is written in a horoscope? Gadadhar's elder brother was conversant with astrological calculations, but could he prevent his own death?

Let us keep astrology aside. Let us concentrate on what can be regarded as a REAL marriage. A REAL MARRIAGE is made in heaven.

Gadadhar's mother Chandramoni Devi had got the news that his youngest son Gadai, who had been installed as the priest in the

Dakshineswar Kali temple had been behaving like a madman. His mind had no stability, his behaviour had no consistency. She was extremely upset at this news and had started crying continuously. Her other son Rameshwar came running to her and hearing everything from her came to Dakshineswar and took Gadai along with him back to Kamarpukur. An exorcist (*ojha* in Bengali) was called to cure Gadai but there was no positive outcome even after the man tried his best.

Anyway, once he improved a little, the family seniors got together and thought that the best solution could be to get him married. At the instance of his mother, Rameshwar started looking for an eligible bride. Since many people had come to know about Gadadhar's mental instability, nobody was agreeing even to start a negotiation. When Chandra Devi and Rameshwar were fed up, Gadadhar himself asked them, in a *bhava*-inflicted mood to go to Joyrambati and look for the house of Ram Chandra Mukhopadhyay where his would-be-bride is waiting to be betrothed to him. The would-be-bride Sarada, then a five-year old girl, was located by Gadadhar's *spiritual intelligence*, without any special effort. When Gadadhar was twenty-four, they were married. This is an example of a REAL MARRIAGE – a marriage planned and made in heaven. (Reference 24)

REAL Sacrifice

The guest house of Rani Rashmoni was really big. Every day, thousands of visitors, guests, sadhus and sannyasis of different sects and cults used to have a share of the Goddess's *prasadam* in the temple. Rani was a great devotee of the Goddess and was most generous and elaborate in her arrangements for offering *puja* and distributing *prasadam* to those who were present. Nobody used to be deprived of the *prasadam* at lunch time.

Unfortunately, none of those who ate the *prasadam* cleaned up the place where they ate. After the lunch session was over, Sri Sri Ramakrishna will visit the dining hall, collect all the banana leaves (*prasadam* used to be served on banana leaves), make a heap of them, put the heap on his own head, carry it to the bank of the River Ganges and throw it on the garbage bin. This way, he used to keep the temple dining hall clean. He firmly believed that this was a *REAL sacrifice* clearing his path towards coming very close to his Mother Goddess. The banana leaves carried the remnants of the *prasadam* made in her honour and offered to her. So, Ramakrishna's gesture was a symbol of his *service* to the Mother Goddess.

Thakur used to clean the temple precincts in the dead of night so that nobody could see him. He loved to work silently and away from everyone's sight (Reference 25)

REAL Teacher

Sri Sri Ramakrishna was never interested in rote learning, but he was a keen learner to know about all ways and means of getting access to the *Divine*. He had, with great interest, taken lessons on different thoughts & concepts under Hinduism and also on different religions like Christianity, Islam and so on. In this connection, he had taken the help of different teachers; and, some of them were REAL teachers. By the term 'REAL Teacher', I mean someone who recognises the quality of the student and acknowledges her/his superiority where she/he deserves. I'll share two examples from Sri Sri Ramakrishna's life.

Around 40 in age, very fair and good-looking Bhairavi Brahmani came to Dakshineswar to teach Ramakrishna *Tantra Sadhana*. She had got a divine message that there were three most eligible persons to be trained by her, and one of them was Sri Ramakrishna.

Brahmani always used to carry a *salgram shila* – a symbol of Lord Raghubir. She never used to have anything before offering it to the *shila*. One day, she had offered *bhog* to *shila*. Paramhansa arrived there in half-awake state (in *bhava*) and started eating all the food offered to Lord Raghubir. Since Brahmani had *darshan* of Ramakrishna while meditating on Raghubir, she did not mind at such behaviour of him. When Thakur got back to his normal senses, he got very embarrassed and asked her whether he had done anything wrong. Brahmani replied: "You've done the right thing. It's not you but the one who is inside you has done it. I've realised it while immersed in my meditation."

(Was it that whenever Sri Sri Ramakrishna went into a *bhava*, his *soul* became detached from everything worldly and it used to invoke some divine spirit into it so that, without his own knowledge, others started seeing him as a divine figure while meditating? Otherwise, how else it would be possible!!)

The Brahmani was so overwhelmed that she had got the *darshan* of real Raghubir in Sri Sri Ramakrishna that she started shedding tears of happiness. She went to the Holy River Ganges with tears in her eyes and the *salgram shila* (which she had been worshipping all these years) in her hand and threw it in the flowing water. Showing *honour* to a student is the sign of REAL TEACHERSHIP.

Naga sannyasi Totapuri came to teach *Vedanta* to Sri Sri Ramakrishna. In order to learn authentic *Vedanta*, Ramakrishna had to go for *sannyas*. He had first taken the consent of his Mother Goddess Kali. However, since Ramakrishna's biological mother Chandra Devi was alive and around, and she would be extremely upset at such a decision of her beloved son, the procedure had to be performed most secretly. Totapuri had taken all steps for a secret *puja* and they faced no problem while following the ritualistic procedure. The final step of learning authentic *Vedanta* is to do meditation leading to *nirvikalpa samadhi* where your mind becomes absolutely zero-thought, zero-image, as the essence of *Vedanta* is in the *nirakar* (shapeless, formless) concept. Ramakrishna started on his meditative journey but, every time, he was trying to attain the zero-thought, zero-image state of mind, he was getting the thoughts and images of his Mother Goddess Kali. Totapuri got very annoyed that what kind of a *sadhak* was Ramakrishna that he was not able to remove the thoughts and images of Goddess Kali from his mind. Being a *Vedantist*, he was a strong disbeliever of worshipping images. He picked up a sharp-edged piece of broken glass from the bushes nearby, pressed it hard on the forehead of Ramakrishna, tried to divert his Goddess-filled mind to the excruciating pain caused by the sharp-edged glass. It was an effective trigger for the Paramhansa – as he was able to concentrate. Totapuri locked the door and went off, hoping that Ramakrishna will knock when he woke up from his *samadhi*. From time to time, he came to check up if Thakur's *samadhi* had broken – but not a chance!! After waiting for three long days, Totapuri himself opened the door of the room where Thakur was meditating, chanted *mantras* to wake him up. He had his own ways of checking whether Thakur was in real *nirvikalpa samadhi* or not; and, he was more than convinced that it was absolutely genuine. The aged naga *sannyasi* was amazed that the *nirvikalpa samadhi* state which he had taken so many years to attain, Ramakrishna could attain it so easily. This very incident convinced him about the highly advanced spiritual state of Saint Ramakrishna. He acknowledged to his student that he was really someone very special. That is the sign of a REAL TEACHER who acknowledges something very special in his students and says so. (Reference 26)

REAL Knowledge

What we see and hear around us are all *maya.* 'REAL Knowledge' is something else as the following example will indicate.

It was a full moon night in autumn. The whole place was bathed in the glow of moonlight. Ramakrishna, in a *bhava,* suddenly asked his elder cousin Haladhari, who had been employed as the priest in the Kali temple for some time: "Is it full moon or a moonless night today?" Haladhari snapped at him: "I've never seen such a stupid before".

Although Haladhari was well-versed in the *shastras*, Thakur had REAL Knowledge. A *sadhak* who is REALLY knowledgeable, to him, there is no distinction between anything – day and night, good and bad. The diversity of *Mother Nature* disappears. (Reference 27)

REAL Religion

Sri Sri Ramakrishna's Epigraph

"I have practised all religions – Hinduism, Islam, Christianity – and I have also followed the paths of the different Hindu sects. I have found that it is the same God toward whom all are directing their steps, though along different paths. You must try all beliefs and traverse all the different ways once. Wherever I look, I see men quarrelling in the name of religion – Hindus, Mohammedans, Brahmos, Vaishnavas, and the rest. But they never reflect that He who is called Krishna is also called Siva, and bears the name of the Primal Energy, Jesus, and Allah as well – the same Rama with a thousand names. A lake has several ghats. At one, the Hindus take water in pitchers and call it 'jal'; at another the Mussalmans take water in leather bags and call it 'pani'. At a third the Christians call it 'water'. Can we imagine that it is not 'jal', but only 'pani' or 'water'? How ridiculous! The substance is One under different names, and everyone is seeking the same substance; only climate, temperament, and name create differences. Let each man follow his own path. If he sincerely and ardently wishes to know God, peace be unto him! He will surely realize Him."

— *Ramakrishna*

References

[1] "Ma Go Ashru Jeno Mor" Devotional Song of Ramakrishna Mission, YouTube.

[2] Dilip Kumar Ghosh, *Sri Sri Ramakrishna Punthi: Ek Alshay Srishti*; (In Bengali), Kolkata: Sahityasree, 2024, pp. 108–112.

[3] "Prahlada" – *Wikipedia.*

[4] "An Extraordinary Tale of Sri Ramakrishna on How Firm Faith Can Make Even Impossibles Possible", Video Presentation on You Tube (In Bengali), *Spiritual Bulletin.*

[5] "Crossing the Red Sea" – *Wikipedia.*

[6] "Moses and the Red Sea: Stories from the Bible – Crossing the Red Sea – Jesus Christ" Video Presentation in English in YouTube, *Geethanjali Kids.*

[7] "God parts the Red Sea – Moses and Israelites Crossing – Animated Bible Stories" – Video Presentation in English in YouTube, *My First Bible.*

[8] Dilip Kumar Ghosh, *Sri Sri Ramakrishna Punthi: Ek Akshay Shristi*, (In Bengali) Kolkata: Sahityasree, 2023, pp. 206–207.

[9] Sri M, *Sri Sri Ramakrishna Kathamrita (Akhanda)* (In Bengali), Kolkata: Ashoke Book Agency, 2022–23, pp. 43–44 and p. 12.

[10] Daniel Z. Lieberman MD & Michael E. Long, *The Molecule of More: How a Single Chemical in Your Brain Drives Love, Sex, and Creativity –*

and Will Determine the Fate of the Human Race, Dallas, TX: BenBella Books, Inc. 2018.

[11] Dr Anna Lembke, *Dopamine Nation: Finding Balance in the Age of Indulgence*, London: Headline Publishing Group, 2021.

[12] "The Three Temperaments", *TantraMag*, 6th January 2016.

[13] "Kapalika" – *Wikipedia.*

[14] "Spiritual Intelligence" – *Wikipedia.*

[15] "Prahlada" – *Wikipedia.*

[16] Devdutt Pattanaik, "Kali and her tongue", The Times of India, 12th December 2011.

[17] "'Error Neurons' Play Role in How Brain Processes Mistakes", *Cedars Sinai*, Los Angeles, USA, 4th December 2018.

[18] "Phalaharini Soroshi Puja by Sri Ramakrishna", *Yang Bharat*, anilkarn78.wixsite.com

[19] Dilip Kumar Ghosh, *Sri Sri Ramakrishna Punthi: Ek Akshay Shristi* (In Bengali), Kolkata: Sahityasree, 2023, p. 32.

[20] Dilip Kumar Ghosh, *Sri Sri Ramakrishna Punthi: Ek Akshay Shristi* (In Bengali), Kolkata: Sahityasree, 2023, p. 215.

[21] Dilip Kumar Ghosh, *Sri Sri Ramakrishna Punthi: Ek Akshay Shristi* (In Bengali), Kolkata: Sahityasree, 2023, p. 28–29

[22] Paul J. Zak, The Moral Molecule: How Trust Works, New York: Plume (Penguin Group), 2013.

[23] Dilip Kumar Ghosh, *Sri Sri Ramakrishna Punthi: Ek Akshay Shristi*, (In Bengali), Kolkata: Sahityasree, 2023, pp. 200–201.

[24] Dilip Kumar Ghosh, *Sri Sri Ramakrishna Punthi: Ek Akshay Shristi* (In Bengali), Kolkata: Sahityasree, 2023, p. 49.

[25] Dilip Kumar Ghosh, *Sri Sri Ramakrishna Punthi: Ek Akshay Shristi* (In Bengali), Kolkata: Sahityasree, 2023, pp. 54–55.

[26] Dilip Kumar Ghosh, *Sri Sri Ramakrishna Punthi: Ek Akshay Shristi*, (In Bengali), Kolkata: Sahityasree, 2023, pp. 73–74; and pp. 104–105.

[27] Dilip Kumar Ghosh, *Sri Sri Ramakrishna Punthi: Ek Akshay Shristi* (In Bengali), Kolkata: Sahityasree, 2024, pp. 90–91.

CHAPTER 5

Sri Sri Ramakrishna as a Spiritual Entrepreneur

"If I were asked under what sky the human mind has most fully developed some of its choicest gifts, has most deeply pondered on the greatest problems of life, and has found solutions to some of them which will deserve the attention of even those who have studied Plato and Kant, I should point out India."

—***Max Muller****, German-born British philologist and orientalist (1823–1900)*

"Religions are all man-made. Each claims itself to be the BEST! If Ramakrishna had not descended on this planet, who would have settled the conflicts between the different religions? The *Avatar* used to say: 'Every religion is REAL. Every religion is TRUE. I've followed & practised each of them, and I'm totally convinced about the common link between them that binds them together. Each religion has a specific path to be followed and all different paths finally meet in one GOD.' This unification of all religions was possible only because of him. He had followed and practised each of them in his own life and only then come to such an understanding."

—***Dilip Kumar Ghosh****, Sri Sri Ramakrishna Punthi: Ek Akshay Shristi, (In Bengali) Kolkata: Sahityasree, 2023, pp. 175–176.*

Spiritual Entrepreneurship

Ever since I was a child, the most favourite spot for me in the Kolkata Alipo.re Zoo was a well-spread watershed, surrounded by banyan and other large trees. I used to sit there munching peanuts with black salt. The trees had temporary nests of seasonal birds who had flown from far-flung places across the Himalayas to make their temporary sojourns.

The lake was full of ducks of all kinds who would be in the water most of the time occasionally coming up on the shores flipping their wings to shed off the drops of water if any. I used to watch them with full focus to see how clean they were. I wish, we humans could shed off the enemies of our mind as easily as them – the *'ripus'* – lust, anger, greed, infatuation, delusion, arrogance, and jealousy.

In one corner, away from the ordinary ducks were a few snow-white swans – so beautiful. They were mostly in water with their large bodies.

In a far distant corner, there were a couple of black swans – with jade black silky body and blood-red beaks, reminding me of our Hindu Goddess Kali who has a black body with a bloody red tongue protruding out.

If you want to be an entrepreneur of any kind – literary, musical, choreographical, cinematographic, business, professional, medical, therapeutic, even SPIRITUAL (like Sri Sri Ramakrishna), find out your BLACK SWAN qualities – whether you have any unique SKILL, INTELLIGENCE or TALENT which makes you totally different from others. Find out how you can make it marketable to others, find out where your market would be.

Lord Jesus Christ, Prophet Muhammad, Bhagwan Buddha, Bhagwan Sri Sri Chaitanya, Srila Prabhupada (founder of ISKCON), and Sri Sri Ramakrishna (founder of a totally new approach to spirituality) were all SPIRITUAL ENTREPRENEURS.

Find out your 'niche' which will be marketable. If you are a creative painter, hung up your paintings for sale but there are no buyers/takers, then you are not an Art Entrepreneur.

Sri Sri Ramakrishna, a totally illiterate person, underwent training in different religions and different schools of Hinduism so that he can discover a common link which he started MARKETING through his excellent simple communication packed with puranic and other tales.

Lord Jesus Christ was an excellent marketer. He used his healing power to build faith in him.

Unless you can build a bridge of Oxytocin between yourself and your potential customer, you cannot last as an entrepreneur.

A real entrepreneur converts a potential customer into a customer, a customer into a client, a client into an advocate, and an advocate into an evangelist.

Sri Sri Ramakrishna used to turn his devotees into evangelists. All the monks of his order are evangelists today.

More about Spiritual Entrepreneurship

One who develops a new school of spirituality, I call that person a spiritual entrepreneur. The Middle-Eastern and the South-Central parts of Asia have been the breeding grounds of *spiritual entrepreneurship.* The founder of Judaism Abraham and the founder of Christianity Lord Jesus, were both spiritual entrepreneurs from the Middle-East. So were Prophet Muhammad, the founder of Islam and Prophet Zoroaster, the founder of Zoroastrianism. The Hindu *rishis* who wrote the Vedas and the Upanishads that form the base of Hinduism, Lord Buddha who founded Buddhism, Mahavir – the founder of Jainism, and Guru Nanak, the founder of Sikhism were all spiritual entrepreneurs from India. These breeding grounds of spiritual entrepreneurship were very rich in mineral resources; the Middle-East filthy rich in crude oil; and India rich in all types of mineral resources. Africa and the Americas were unexplored dark continents. India became a target for the Muslim Caliphs of the Middle-East and the Europeans – the Portuguese, the Dutch, the French and the British. Africa and the Americas became targets of the Europeans -all for their rich resources.

Hansman Anthony

Many Portuguese merchants came by the oceanic route to Bengal and settled there. Amongst them were the ancestors of Hansman Anthony (1786–1834). Anthony was interested in music and he was fascinated by Hindustani classical music and also the local *kabigan.* He had a baritone voice and he was keen to pick up *kabigan.* It is said that he had saved a young brahmin widow Soudamini from being *sati*, had a live-in relationship with her rejecting all his European suitors who were all attracted to him for his handsomeness, musical talents and extra-sweet temperament. Soudamini could also sing beautifully and she encouraged him to learn Bengali, Sanskrit shastras, and *kabigan*, which were all based on the *Vaishnava* and the *Shakta* schools of Hinduism.

Anthony formed his own band and started performing in many gatherings sponsored by *zamindars* and Hindu aristocrats, participated regularly in *Kabir Ladai* (fight between two groups of native poets) and won accolades. He came to be known as *Anthony Firingi*.

Anthony's live-in partner Soudamini used to perform pujas regularly. Both of them wished to set up a Kali temple in Central Calcutta. Anthony mobilised funds, purchased a land in Bowbazar, and built the Kali temple which is known as *Firingi Kalibari*. It is one of the most popular Kali temples of Kolkata now with many devotees offering regular worship there.

I would regard Anthony Firingi as a *spiritual entrepreneur* as he being a Portuguese Christian, got devoted to Hinduism and set up a temple for Kali worship in Central Calcutta.

Sri Sri Ramakrishna (1836–1886) was born just two years after Anthony Firingi breathed his last, but when he left this planet, he had already laid the foundation of his worldwide spiritual enterprise with the responsibilities for translating his dream into reality already allocated to his apostles.

I have found seven features common to both of them:

- Both had lost their fathers very early in life, were brought up by their widowed mothers.
- Both were extremely dynamic in their own special ways and were prepared to take great risks.
- Both had spent their lives on the banks of the Holy River Ganges.
- Both were great devotees of Goddess Kali.
- Both believed in the bests of all religions.
- Both were very proficient in singing and dancing. Both had

a beautiful voice and displayed most graceful way of dance movements.

- Both did not have any offspring as that would have interfered with their *spiritual entrepreneurship*.

I am tempted to share the English translation of a very famous Bengali song by Anthony Firingi:

"Christ and Krishna, there is no difference, brother.
Only by name people differ, no one listens...
Christ and Krishna, there is no difference, brother.
Christ and Krishna, there is no difference, brother.

My God, who is also the Hindu Hari...
Look there, Shyam (another name for Krishna), is standing.
My human life will be fulfilled if I can get the red feet (a Reference to divine grace).
Christ and Krishna, there is no difference, brother.
Only by name people differ, no one listens...
Christ and Krishna, there is no difference, brother...
Christ and Krishna, there is no difference, brother...
Christ and Krishna...
There is no difference, brother...
There is no difference, brother.
There is no difference, brother."

Firingi Kalibari, a historic temple in Kolkata, India, is dedicated to the Hindu goddess Kali. Located on B.B. Ganguly Street, the temple dates back to the early 18th century. Its name, "Firingi," meaning "foreigner," is derived from its association with Anthony Firingi, a Portuguese poet and devotee of Kali who significantly contributed to the temple's establishment and upkeep. Anthony Firingi, born Hensman Anthony, was known for his devotion and his efforts to promote the worship of Kali among the local Bengali population. The temple has since become a significant cultural and religious landmark, reflecting the syncretic heritage of Kolkata, where diverse influences have historically influenced it to qualify as a spiritual landmark in the whole of India, although Varanasi is the country's spiritual capital. (References 1–7)

Ramakrishna's Spiritual Entrepreneurship

As an entrepreneur, what was Sri Sri Ramakrishna's *product* that he wanted to market. It was *Humanistic Religion* – that there is God in every human being irrespective of his religion, community, caste and creed. What was his *market*? His *market* was the whole world.

He was an illiterate person. He had no idea of the principles or techniques of marketing and sales. But, he had a most mesmerising way of communicating establishing each key concept with a *puranic* or folk tale or with the help of his own experiences. He used most simple language, without any jargons at all (which his biographer Mahendra Nath Gupta had described as *kathamrita* – the nectar of communication).

Like a most effective marketer, he used to follow this step-by-step procedure: conversion of a 'potential customer' into a 'customer', a 'customer' into a 'client' ('repeat buyer'), a 'client' into an 'advocate' (who vouches for the marketer and his product), and, an 'advocate' into an 'evangelist' (who becomes the voice for the marketer and his product). There are umpteen examples of his such marketing strategies in Ramakrishna literature. (References 8–10)

References

[1] "Anthony Firingi – Bengali Full Movie" – YouTube

[2] "Jaatishwar" – *Wikipedia.*

[3] "Firinghi Kalibari" – *Wikipedia.*

[4] "Kolkata Firingi Kalibari History" – Video on YouTube.

[5] Madan Bandyopadhyay, *Kobiyal Antoni Firingi,* (In Bengali) (2nd Edition) Calcutta: Satyabrata Library, 29th Sraban, 1365 (Bengali Year).

[6] "Anthony Firingi" – *Wikipedia.*

[7] Akshay Kumar Maitra, *Firingi Banick* (In Bengali), (1st Edition), Calcutta: Gurudas Chattopadhyay & Sons, Sraban, 1329 (Bengali Year).

[8] Sri M, *Sri Sri Ramakrishna Kathamrita (Akhanda)* (In Bengali), Kolkata: Ashoke Book Agency, Reprint, 2022–23.

[9] Swami Saradananda, *Sri Sri Ramakrishna Lilaprasanga (1st Part)* (In Bengali), Kolkata: Udbodhan Karjalaya, 1993.

[10] Swami Saradananda, *Sri Sri Ramakrishna Lilaprasanga (2nd Part)* (In Bengali), Kolkata: Udbodhan Karjalaya, 1991.

CHAPTER 6

Sri Sri Ramakrishna & The 'Black Swan' Concept

The 'Black Swan' Concept

The *Black Swan* concept is a metaphor that describes an event: that comes as a surprise, has a major to very major impact, and is often inappropriately rationalised after the fact with the benefit of hindsight.

The term is based on a Latin expression which presumed that *black swans* did not exist. The expression was used until 1697 when Dutch mariners saw them, by chance, in Australia. Swans are natives of Australia. After the Dutch discovery, the term was reinterpreted to mean an unforeseen and consequential event. (Reference 1)

Nassim Nicholas Taleb (Reference 2) has defined it to include 'high-profile, hard-to-predict, and extremely rare events that are beyond the realm of normal expectations in history, science, finance, and technology. The event is a surprise and has a major effect. According to Taleb, the COVID-19 pandemic was not a *black swan*, as it was expected with great certainty that a global pandemic will eventually take place. Instead, it is considered a *white swan* event. A *white swan* event has a major effect but it is the outcome of somebody's or some other event's intervention. (References 3 & 4)

If Sri Sri Ramakrishna's descendance on this planet was not expected or predicted by anyone human, then we must regard it as a *black swan* event. (Although a reader might argue that Gadadhar's father Khsudiram Chatterjee had witnessed a dream, while sojourning in Gaya, where Lord Vishnu had appeared and told him that he will be born in the Chatterjee family as his son.) Nobody (including Rani Rashmoni and her son-in-law) had expected Ramakrishna to emerge as an *avatar*. Even Bhairavi Brahmani and Naga Sannyasi Totapuri as well as Jatadhari and other *sadhaks* could not comprehend what the REAL RAMAKRISHNA was.

Swami Vivekananda was a *white swan* as he was a better than normal but not an extraordinary person; he was transformed entirely by Sri Sri Ramakrishna. If Ramakrishna would not have intervened, he would have remained Narendra Nath Dutta, a smart lawyer or attorney.

However, swans – both of white and black varieties are extremely fragile, as they have brittle bones. They have weaker bones than other animals that are vulnerable to breakage (Reference 5). One can see how valid it is in both Ramakrishna and Vivekananda's case. Ramakrishna got throat cancer (for reason unknown) and within only a few years after he started feeling pain in his throat, he died on 16th August 1886 at the age of 50 only. (Reference 6). Swami Vivekananda suffered from *asthma* and *diabetes*, but was reportedly in good health on the day of his death. He passed away on 4th July 1902, somewhat mysteriously. While according to his disciples, he attained *mahasamadhi*, it was the rupture of a blood vessel that is reported to have killed him. Apparently, it was a case of heart attack. At the time of his death, his age was only 39 years, 5 months, and 24 days. (Reference 7)

'The Monk of a Man' by renowned Bengali writer Shankar lists insomnia, liver, and kidney diseases, malaria, migraine, diabetes, and heart ailments as some of the 31 health problems that the Swami faced in the course of his life. His is the right example of the saying that: "The body is the temple of diseases". Vivekananda had tried different modes of treatment ranging from allopathic, homeopathic to ayurvedic and had also taken advice from all kinds of quasi-medical experts from various countries. (Reference 8)

Is it a fact that transformed *white swans* are more fragile and brittle than inborn *black swans*?

It would be a nice topic for further research provided statistically valid sample size is available which would be a far cry. However, my speculation is that *Ramakrishna* had transformed him for a few specific purposes with pre-determined timelines. When Vivekananda fulfilled those purposes, there was no reason for him to live any longer as, being a *sannyasi*, he had no family and there was no need for him to live any longer in a mortal life.

'Paramhansa' & 'Black Swan'

'Hansa'/'Hans' means 'Swan'.
'Paramhansa' means the 'Great Swan'.

The 'Paramhansa' concept is popular in Hinduism. The swan is most comfortable in water, but although it may not be so comfortable in land, moving on the land is not inconvenient for it. It can 'manage'. Similarly, a 'Paramhansa', which is a religious-theological title of honour applied to a Hindu spiritually enlightened teacher, is most comfortable in the spiritual realm, he may not be so much at home with householders, school & college going youngsters, and old widows and widowers of all religions, communities, castes and creeds. *Avatar* Ramakrishna was at that level – so I place him on a higher pedestal and compare him to the very rare 'Black Swan'.

'Paramhansa' Yogananda, in his popular book *The Autobiography of a Yogi* stated that the 'Swan' mythologically represented the vehicle or mount of Lord Brahma, the Creator. '*Hansa*' is a symbol of spiritual discrimination. '*Hansa*' literally means 'I am He' and has a vibrating connection with the incoming and outgoing breath. Thus, with your every breath, you can feel the existence of your life-force. 'I am He' can also be interpreted as 'I' (Jivatma) as a part of 'He' (Paramatma).

The *Paramhansa* Upanishad is one of the 108 (the sacred number) Upanishadic Hindu scriptures, attached to the *Atharvaveda*. It is classified as one of the *Sannyasa Upanishads*.

As per *Vishnu Sahasranama*, 'Paramhansa' is a form of Lord Vishnu who imparted *Vedas* to Lord Brahma in the form of a DIVINE SWAN.

Paramhansa Yogananda was a *sannyasi*. Sri Sri Ramakrishna took *sannyas* from the Naga Sannyasi Totapuri much later, that too most secretly so that his biological mother Chandra Devi must not have known. Otherwise, Ramakrishna was a celibate '*grihi*'. He was beyond the level of a 'Paramhansa'. That is why my perception of him was that of the very rare 'Black Swan'.

Kabir (1398–1518) was a spiritual entrepreneur who advocated unity of religions and he very much succeeded in casting his shadow in Hinduism, Sikhism, and Islam – especially in Sufism.

The 'Swan' concept was very dear to Kabir's heart. His famous bhajan 'Hans Akela Ud Jayega' was sung by many top vocalists including the classical giant Pt. Kumar Gandharva and Bhajan Samrat Anup Jalota.

After reading this piece whether your goal is to attain the 'Hans' state which means liberation from the '*Sada Ripu's*: Desire (Kam/ Kamona), Anger (Krodh), Greed (Lobh), Moha (Infatuation as in 'flimsy' love affairs which help the lovers earn the cheap neurochemical 'Dopamine'), Mad (Stupid Ego/Vanity); and Matsarya (Envy – as happens in a culture of competition as we have everywhere today).

Make a periodic review of your progress. This is, what I call 'Spiritual/ Soul Development'. You will not achieve it by going to religious shrines and offering worships at churches, mosques, temples, gurdwaras and monasteries. Spirituality and Religiousness are miles apart from each other.

Can Swans Sing?

Unfortunately, although they use a variety of sounds to express their emotions and feelings, they cannot sing.

However, there is a myth called 'Swansong' in the western world which says that the swans can anticipate when they are going to die and as death approaches, they sing beautiful songs – as if, (it is my speculation) they can visualise the 'after-death' future that their soul will enter into a most peaceful and tranquil domain much different from the earth where they lived their past life. For this to come true (this is again my speculation) when they anticipate that death is near, they come up on the land and shake their wings a number of times to ensure all drops of water and water-weeds have fallen off – as if they have got rid of all the 6 Enemies of the Mind – the '*Sada Ripus*'. They know very well that even if some *Ripu* remains in them, they will not be able to come out of the birth-death-rebirth cycle. Swans really have SPIRITUAL qualities. (References 9, 10 & 11)

In Greek mythology, swans are associated with the Sun God Apollo who is also the god of archery, music, dance, truth, healing of diseases, poetry and many more.

In Hindu mythology also, the swan is the vehicle or Goddess Saraswati who represents true knowledge & learning, all arts including music, dancing, drama, literature, poetry and fine arts and sculpture.

My Black Swan Sri Sri Ramakrishna could sing and dance very well with perfect pronunciation melody and rhythm. He could also act very well from his boyhood days. My White Swan Vivekananda was a trained dhrupad singer and pakhawaz player and a great orator. Both were dream children of Goddess Saraswati.

Like swans, both of them could anticipate the coming of their death and entered into the 'Samadhi Brain State' which led to '*Mahasamadhi*'. (Reference 12)

Whether their Souls sang their swansongs, I don't know. Shall be very happy if anyone of you could enlighten me.

The 'Swan Effect'

Swans are spiritual birds. A black swan is at the height of spirituality. A white swan is a little less, but still much advanced than an ordinary duck or a goose. (Reference 13)

When they leave the water, at times, and come up to the ground, they shake off all water drops, weeds, dust and dirt from their feathers. It is a reflex activity for them.

In the case of humans, the *Sada Ripu* – the Six Enemies of the Mind are like drops of water, weeds, dirt and dust. (References 14 & 15)

How many of us are consciously endeavouring to reduce/eradicate them? If you are, then you are a duck or a goose amongst other mundane humans. You may not have swan-like spiritual qualities.

In humans, all the six *ripus* (enemies of the mind) are related to the 'gross body' ('*sthula sharira*'). If your 'gross body' is too dominant then your 'subtle body' ('*sukshma sarira*') gets suppressed and subdued. You have '*poshu bhava*' according to *Tantric* concepts. (References 16 & 17)

Just see. *Kam* (desire/lust) is related to your body. *Krodh* (anger) gets reflected in your aggressive body language. *Lobh* (greed) is related to your tongue and stomach. *Moha* (infatuation) is related to your gross body as your biological markers show a sign of excitement when you meet a person to whom you are infatuated. *Mad* (Ego/Vanity) is certainly related to your gross body as when you dress up in elegant/ expensive clothes and accessories, you are showing off to others that you are better off. Buying a new gadget, furniture, flat, or car, landing up a better job, getting double/triple promotion and talking about it to others is certainly your ego-display. *Matsarya* (jealousy/envy) in extreme cases, ends up in physical fight to prove that 'might is right'.

Sri Sri Ramakrishna used to share a slice of his Golden Soul with his eligible disciples to produce this 'Swan Effect' as a cleansing/purification strategy – and it used to work extremely well.

You have no *avatar* near you. You will have to go for the 'Swan Effect' yourself. Just take the least serious enemy of your mind first. Make a time-bound plan (3 months) to reduce/eradicate it. Keep the timeframe 3 months only – neither more, nor less. Do not take more than one '*ripu*' at a time. Work out the reduction/eradication strategies – implement them and check the progress – visualise your success that you have got rid of that '*ripu*' – check with your near and dear ones whether they have also found any improvement in you. This way by adopting the ordinary duck/goose strategy, your target should be to become at least a White Swan.

To implement the 'Swan Effect' for your spiritual development/ refinement, take '*Moha/Maya*' (infatuation/attachment) for example.

When Rani Rashmoni's son-in-law Mathur Babu died in Kalighat, Sri Sri Ramakrishna did not visit him as although he liked Mathur, he was NOT ATTACHED to him. When a devotee asked him whether Mathur Babu will be reborn, Thakur said promptly: 'Of course, he will be reborn as a more wealthy landlord as in his present life, he could not get detached from his love of assets – fixed, movable and liquid.

My father (with all due respect to him) had a fancy for large limousines. He had acquired the latest model of American Studebaker Commander and was ATTACHED to it. It also satisfied his 'Mad' ('Ego') as people appreciated when he drove to the High Court and the Calcutta Club. When he left this planet, did he take his big automobile with him to the other world? In fact, there he does not need any vehicle as in his subtle body he can easily travel through an iron or a stone wall or any barrier. Anyway, like Mathur he must have been born to own much larger and more modern models of cars in his present life, if there is one.

Sri Sri Ramakrishna loved flowers. He had a beautiful flower garden behind the Kali temple in Dakshineswar. But he had never any feeling of ownership of the flowers. He loved flowers for their divine beauty. Appreciation of beauty is a spiritual quality. He appreciated the beautiful jade black bare body of Goddess Kali and the milk-white bare body of Lord Shiva not because of any '*Moha*' or '*Maya*'.

If you have little children or grandchildren, don't get ATTACHED to them. Appreciate their beauty as products of Mother Nature. They may share your genes in their cells which constitutes only 10 percent of their personality, the bulk 90 % comes from their microbiome which is not your gift to them. Besides, their souls have come from outside – which may not vibe with your souls. That is the reason why Ramakrishna was against having kids.

References

[1] David Haworth, "Friday essay: a rare bird – how Europeans got the black swan so wrong", *the conversation.com*. Retrieved 28th March 2024 (original 10th June 2021).

[2] Nassim Nicholas Taleb, *The Black Swan: The Impact of the Highly Improbable*, London: Penguin, 2nd Edition, 2010.

[3] "The Pandemic Isn't A Black Swan, but a Portent of a More Fragile Global System", *The New Yorker*, 21st April 2020.

[4] "Black swan theory" – *Wikipedia.*

[5] Paige Yates, "Swan", *biology dictionary*. Last updated 2nd November 2020.

[6] "Ramakrishna" – *Wikipedia.*

[7] "Remembering Swami Vivekananda: Timeline of spiritual guide who inspired generations", *India Today,* New Delhi, Updated 4th July 2020.

[8] HT Correspondent, Kolkata, "Swami Vivekananda suffered from 31 ailments", *Hindustan Times,* 6th January 2013.

[9] 'Swan Song' – *Wikipedia.*

[10] 'Six Enemies of the Mind (Shad-ripu)" *Yoga with Subhash.*

[11] 'Arishadvargas' – *Wikipedia.*

[12] 'Mahasamadhi' – *Yogapedia,* Last updated 21st December 2023.

[13] 'Black swan theory' – *Wikipedia.*

[14] 'Six Enemies of the Mind (Shad-ripu)" *Yoga with Subhash*

[15] 'Arishadvargas' – *Wikipedia*

[16] 'Three Bodies Doctrine' – *Wikipedia*

[17] 'The Three Temperaments' – *TantraMag,* 6th January 2016.

CHAPTER 7

Sri Sri Ramakrishna as a Reader & Judge of People

The 'Six Enemies of the Mind'

Sada Ripu are all resources of someone who is of a demonic or *asuric* nature. Slaying the demon or *asura* means overcoming the 'Six Enemies of the Mind'. That is why Devi Durga (who killed Mahishasura) and Ma Kali (who killed a number of ferocious demons) are so popularly worshipped especially in Bengal.

However, demons, *asuras, rakshasas* are mythical characters. In humans, they represent the Tantra's '*Poshu*' and '*Veera/Naro*' *bhavas.* When you come to think of it, the root cause of such propensities is lack of 'Authentic/True Knowledge' which is a characteristic of the '*Divya*' *bhava.*

Lack of 'Authentic/True Knowledge' means your Stupid Ego is active. Your Stupid Ego makes you feel 'I am the Boss' – you are the '*Karta*' – the 'Master'.

If you have 'Authentic/True Knowledge', you will know that you are not the 'Master' – you are the 'Master's 'Servant' – '*Dasa*'.

If you are earning your livelihood through employment, being an 'employee', you are the 'servant' of the organisation where you are employed.

If you are a product or service provider through your own business, you are the 'servant' of all your customers.

If you are a teacher/professor, you are the servant of the school/college/university where you are teaching.

But inside in the core of your mind, you have the '*Karta*/Master' ego lying subconsciously. So you are in a continuous conflict between the 'Master' in your subconscious and the 'Servant' in your 'Conscious'. This conflict is draining out your precious physical and mental energy, affecting your health.

Sri Sri Ramakrishna hated the 'Master' role. He, very rarely, played the '*Guru*' role. He believed in 'mass teaching/learning' (*loka shiksha*). He was very happy and contented being the servant ('*dasa*') of Goddess Kali. He never took a step without consulting Goddess Kali whom he regarded as the 'Great Master'.

How can you play the '*dasa*' role in your family. I will tell you how I always try to play.

I take full care of my aged (81) and ailing wife by being her complete care-giver and service-provider. With her, I become her 'AYAH'. I have been playing this role since 2018 when I gave up my outside professional activities. I had not known Sri Sri Ramakrishna then so deeply and thoroughly as I know him now. He says: 'At home, with your family, you behave like a rich man's/woman's maid servant. Just like a maid servant allows the bulk of her mind to be occupied with the thoughts of the family of her master/mistress and only a slice devoted to the thoughts of her own family and folks in her village, similarly you devote the bulk of your mind to the care-giving work for your family regarding it as GOD's WORK, while devoting a slice to doing spiritual work. Make your home your temple and the people you serve gods and goddesses'.

Your '*Karta*' ('Master') ego keeps you away from doing any household work in your own house. I have recently come across a very senior novelist screaming at his sweeper for not doing his work properly (I myself clean the two toilets in my flat), shouting at the temporary lady cook for late-coming (my Personal Secretary Pervez Alam has employed a lady cook Rashmoni – which was the name of the founder of the Dakshineswar Kali temple where Sri Ramakrishna was employed as the priest for some time – who is so punctual that you can figure out the clock time when she comes and goes – I can't cook).

In India, we have a 'mastery'-oriented social culture – 'mastery' meaning 'control' over others. I hardly come across anybody in my daily life now who wants to have 'mastery' in her/his own field/domain. My role models are Satyajit Ray and Pt. Ravi Shankar who had become 'maestros' by reaching the peak in their respective domains. My role models are Dr Devi Shetty and the Master Chef Sanjeev Kapur. My role models are the superstars Uttam Kumar and Amitabh Bachchan. I am not happy being anything less. My endeavour is to have total control over myself – being a 'Master' of myself – to be a 'Maestro' in my own domain.

Cleaning your own house, washing your own clothes manually, cleaning up the pots and pans, watering your plants will keep you physically fit and will help you to earn 'Dopamine' which otherwise you may be inclined to earn from junk food, playing cards, consuming alcohol, drinking coffee or from nicotine.

You will be amazed to know that you can manage to become a maestro in your field/domain, you can come out of the birth-death-rebirth roller coaster ride and become a 'MASTER' in space to guide others who need your advice. Sri Sri Ramakrishna was an '*avatar*' and an '*avatar*' is a 'Supermaster'.

The idea is not entirely mine – I have borrowed the basics from Dr Brian Weiss, MD – the propounder and practitioner of PAST LIFE THERAPY. (References 1, 2 & 3)

In my very rough estimation, very few (not more than 2 to 5%) people that I know now are trying to attain MASTERY to become MAESTROs in their respective domains to get out of the birth-death-rebirth roller coaster ride.

Reading People from their *Aura*

Aura is the 'energy field' that surrounds a living body – in fact, any living organism like a tree, a plant, a leaf, or a flower. It is invisible to common people, but visible to mystics, psychics, and clairvoyants.

Just like we have our 'physical' bodies, we have 'non-physical' bodies too that layer around our human form. In Hindu gods and goddesses, the *halo* around – particularly, their head, is nothing but the representation of their *auras*. In highly spiritual people at the moment of their highly spiritual brain state, the *aura* sometimes becomes visible – as has been mentioned in Sri Sri Ramakrishna's case in Bengali Ramakrishna literature. (Reference 4)

The *aura* is nothing but the seven colours of the rainbow and, *yogic* and *tantric* scriptures associate those with the seven *chakras*. The VIBGYOR of the rainbow is associated with the *chakras* in a reverse manner – ROYGBIV. That means, the lowest/bottommost chakra *'Muladhar'* is 'Red', *'Swadhisthan* is 'Orange' and *'Manipura'* is 'Yellow'. Can you figure out that all the *Sadaripus* (the 'Six Enemies of the Mind') are related to these three *chakras* from the navel downwards; and they represent the *Tantric 'poshu' bhava*. The *'Anahata' chakra* at the 'heart' level is related to the 'Green' colour. It represents emotions and thus is a characteristic feature of the *'naro' bhava*. The *'Visuddhi' chakra* at the 'throat' level is related to the 'Blue' colour and is an interesting mix of all the three *bhavas*: *'poshu' (slang/abusive language)*, *'naro' (worldly, materialistic, householder's language* – where *'kam'* and *'kanchan'* are very much involved), and *'divya' bhava* (*spiritually flavoured language* – totally free from the 'Six Enemies of the Mind').

[Sri Sri Ramakrishna had the habit of frequently using *slangs/abusive* language although being an *avatar* his forte was the *divya bhava language*. The communicative apparatus and its associated parts as well as the *Visuddhi Chakra* vibrate according to the language in which you express yourself orally.]

The two higher *chakras* are: *'Ajna'* and *'Sahasrar'* – both are very much inside the brain, the first one in between the eyebrows – the 'Third Eye' and the last one above the *brahmatalu* level – being respectively related to the 'Indigo' and 'Violet' colours. *'Ajna'* represents deep intelligence and *'Sahasrar'* – spirituality. These two *chakras* were most active in Sri Sri Ramakrishna. The *Sahasrar Chakra* is not really a part of your body, the way the other six *chakras* are. It floats a little above the centre of your head and connects your physical body to your higher spiritual self. (References 5 & 6)

Now, the *Aura Theory* is like this. Depending on your nature, your *aura* will be of a specific colour. And, with change in your mood, attitude, propensity and so on, your *aura* colour will also change. The more changes that take place in your *aura* colour, it will be more energy-costly for you. That is why, the yogis lead a secluded meditative life. Householders, employees, self-employed and business persons have a fluctuating *aura* as they are saddled with family and work-related problems. I have already written in a few places in my works on Sri Sri Ramakrishna that he had his own strategy and technique for handling a sudden *aura* change by getting into a *bhava samadhi* by losing consciousness.

Vibrational frequencies of the different *chakra*s are: *Muladhar* (Root Chakra – 396 Hz); *Swadhisthan* (Sacral Chakra – 417 Hz); *Manipura* (Solar Plexus Chakra – 528 Hz.); *Anahata* (Heart Chakra – 639 Hz.); *Visuddhi* (Throat Chakra – 741 Hz.); *Ajna* (Third Eye Chakra – 852 Hz.); *Sahasrar* (Crown Chakra – 963 Hz.). Sri Sri Ramakrishna could have possibly felt the frequencies of various people he met and would usually reject those who were in the lower frequency range of 396 – 528 Hz as he would feel that for people belonging to that time has not come yet to be transformed to a higher frequency level. How could he have such powers to read and judge people instinctively? Because, he would, while meeting a person will activate his *Ajna* or *Sahasrar Chakra.* Being at the *Ajna* frequency (852 Hz.), he could tap into his psychic abilities and sense things which are not perceptible by ordinary senses; extra-sensory perception would be called for. When at the *Sahasrar* frequency (963 Hz.), his spiritual side will open up and he would connect himself with Goddess Kali. He would experience a sense of oneness with the Universe. (Reference 7)

Ramakrishna's *Tantra guru* Bhairavi Brahmani had taught him and made him follow, in proper sequence, all the rituals prescribed in sixty-four *tantra*s prevalent in *Bishnukranta.* These were most complicated and difficult rituals which most *sadhak*s fail to complete. Thakur believed that the Mother Goddess had helped him to succeed in pursuing and completing those without any hassle.

As a consequence, Paramhansa's handsomeness had got much enhanced due to the purification and widening of his body's 'energy field' – his *aura*; it was comparable to silvery moonshine. So that people do not start wondering what has suddenly happened to him, Brahmani used to cover his whole body with a scarf. However, the *aura* was so strong and bright, that the scarf could not cover it up. Ramakrishna felt most uncomfortable and he used to pray to the Goddess that he was not longing for any bodily beauty or handsomeness. He prayed to her for taking it away and replace it with divine shine in his *soul.* (Reference 8)

Sri Sri Ramakrishna's Sport (*Leela*) with *Aura*

Ramakrishna, being an *avatar*, could read the *aura* in any object – whether it is steady or moderately fluctuating or fluctuating too much draining out precious biological energy. He had preferences for trees, plants, flowers and people according to the nature of their *auras.*

Narendranath Dutta was a highly intelligent young man; so, he presumably had a 'blue' core *aura*. Ramakrishna did not have to put in much effort to convert him into 'indigo' – he did not have to share a big slice from his own soul. Eventually, in course of a few months, he was converted to 'violet' and got totally transformed.

Most of Ramakrishna's young devotees, who became his apostles later, came with an 'green' *aura*. That means they had pure hearts. Ramakrishna slowly slowly transformed them to 'violet' and that was the time when they left their householder's life and became monks.

Now, let me share an example where Sri Sri Ramakrishna totally rejected a person from touching his feet because, he could possibly see a lower frequency vibration in her. The name of the person was Bhagawati Dasi. She was an old maid in Mathur Babu's household but, in her young age, she didn't have a good character. One day, Bhagawati Dasi was talking to Thakur and then suddenly she touched his feet to offer her respect. Immediately, the *avatar* behaved in a way as if a poisonous scorpion had bitten him. Chanting Gobinda's name, he went to the big pot in the corner of his room which had the Holy water from the Ganges. He sprinkled Ganges water on the portions of his feet which had been touched by the woman. (Reference 9)

Akshay Kumar Sen, author of *Ramakrishna Punthi* writes: "The way Thakur used to behave with me, if it were any other person, he would have never gone to him even if his life was in danger. I used to find so many people touching and massaging his feet, but when I used to extend my hand, he will move his feet away from me and would say – 'It's OK, It's OK'." Actually, Akshay Babu's skin colour was jade-black and his constitution was very thin, emaciated and short-statured. On the whole, he was most ugly-looking. In fact, Swamiji had nick-named him as 'Sankchunni' (in Bengali, meaning an 'ugly female ghost'). He was asthmatic and thus was suffering health-wise; his family life was also not happy. Why the *avatar* did not like him is not clear. I can only speculate that possibly because of his low frequency *aura* and his jade-black complexion (Thakur had been bewitched by only one black complexion and that was Goddess Kali and any other dark-skinned person with a *'naro' bhav* was not acceptable to him) acted as barriers. (Reference 10)

There was a unique case where Sri Sri Ramakrishna had blessed a person by putting his foot right on the head of a person. (Reference 11). The day was Friday, date – 1st January, year – 1886, time – 3 pm. Paramhansa was standing in front of a crowd, underneath a mango tree in the Cossipore Garden House where he had spent the last eight months of his life. He had exposed his *Kalpataru* form to his devotees, as he was feeling a little better in health that afternoon. *Kalpataru* is a very special tree – if you stand under it and ask for anything, you will get it without any hassle. It is Hindu *Puranic* concept.

Thakur had blessed those who were present there by saying: "Let good sense prevail on all of you!" As soon as he finished saying this, he got into the *samadhi* brain state. As soon as he regained his senses, all his devotees began touching his feet, one by one. One of them was Haran Chandra Das, a resident of Beliaghata. When he was about to touch Thakur's feet, he put one foot on Haran's head and transferred his *aura*. All those who were present were awe-struck as they had never seen Ramakrishna blessing somebody in this fashion.

Soon after Thakur Ramakrishna left this planet, Sri Sri Ma Sarada Devi took over and started playing the *Guru Ma* role in right earnest.

Thousands of devotees flocked seeking her *darshan* and blessings. Many also took *diksha* from her. She took over all the virtues and vices, good and bad deeds from them. Many visitors, devotees and monks got the opportunity to touch her feet and get a thin slice of her *aura*.

One of them was especially fortunate whose head she touched with her feet. This lucky person was the first disciple of Swami Vivekananda – Swami Sadananda Maharaj. Sadananda Maharaj was most critically ill in the Mayavati ashram. On receiving this news Ma Sarada travelled to Mayavati with Jogen Ma and Gopal Ma. When she met Sadananda Maharaj, the Swami touched her feet to get her blessings and requested her to bless him as she had blessed him 22 years ago. He had thought that blessing has helped him to lead a monk's life without any hassle. Sarada was quiet. Sadananda said: "Ma, I can feel that time has come for me to bid farewell. I don't know what is waiting for me on the other shore. If you don't bless me the way you had blessed me 22 years ago, I'll put an end to my life here and now at your feet." Ma Sarada was a little perplexed – she possibly couldn't remember how she had blessed Sadananda 22 years ago. There were a few other people in the room. She softly touched his head with both her feet and tears started rolling out from the Swami's eyes. Ma Sarada had fulfilled his wish. This is an example how Sarada Devi transmitted a big slice of her *aura* into Sadananda's body through his head. Maximum *aura* 'leakage' takes place through both the palms and fingers and both feet and toes. That is why in Hindu culture, a senior blesses a junior by touching his head with the palms and fingers or allowing him to touch his feet and toes. *Aura* is shared to the maximum extent by placing the feet and toes on one's head. (Reference 12)

An Interesting *Puranic* Story Related to *Aura*

One day, the milkmaid Gopis came to the bank of the Holy River Yamuna but found that the last boat which they would have taken to cross the river had already left with passengers. They were very worried as to how to return home. While they were just wondering, keeping their milk cans, pots and pans on the ground, the great sage Vedavysa arrived all of a sudden. (Reference 13)

The Gopis saw a ray of hope and told him about their plight and requested him if he could make an alternative arrangement. The sage said that he can but, first of all, he wanted them to offer him something to eat as he was extremely hungry. The Gopis said that all their milk and milk products have already been distributed in the villages; they can offer if there is any left-overs. They scraped every container, every pot and pan and whatever they could find was good enough for one person.

The sage ate to his stomach's content and, satisfied, he addressed the river: "Oh, Holy River! If I've not had anything to eat, please divide yourself and make a passage for us to cross over." The river readily responded; it divided itself into two halves right across and a passage was created. The sage and the Gopis crossed over to the other bank and the river resumed its normal flow. Now, the Gopis, being a little perplexed, asked the sage: "Sir! You ate to your stomach's content but still you told River Yamuna that you'd nothing to eat. How is it possible – we are a little confused. Sir, could you please clarify?"

The great sage said: "We have three bodies – the *gross body* ('*sthula sarira*'), the *subtle body* ('*suksma sarira*'), and the *causal body* ('*karana sarira*'). My *gross body* eats – it has the capacity to get its requisite inputs from the local environment. My *subtle body* gets its energy inputs from the *Paramatma* (the 'cosmos'). Its hunger is not physical – it is spiritual. The *spiritual power storage* contains *Brahma Shakti* – located at the *Brahma Talu* – at the *Sahasrar Chakra* level, where the *aura* colour is *violet* and the vibrational frequency is at its highest. I used this high frequency energy to divide the river and create a passage for us to cross over. My *gross body* had nothing to do with it. Those who generally exist at the level of the three lowest *chakras* – the *Muladhar, Swadhisthana,* and *Manipura* can never think of exercising so much spiritual power." (Reference 14)

Those, who remain at the *Sahasrar chakra* level, have no hunger for any worldly food. Their hunger is for *cosmic energy*. When Thakur Ramakrishna was in the *nirvikalpa samadhi* brain state for three days at a stretch, he had no physical hunger. His spiritual energy supply was coming from the *cosmos*. And, this had utterly surprised the Naga

Sannyasi Totapuri as he had never experienced such a *leela*. (Reference 15)

Narendranath's Failed Attempt to Share a Slice of His *Aura*

In the spiritual domain, very few of those who are pursuing the spiritual path – the *sadhaks*, have the good fortune to acquire the power to transmit spiritual powers to others by exercising willpower and physical touch (sharing a slice of the *aura*).

Sri Sri Ramakrishna had told his close disciples, again and again, that Narendranath (later Swami Vivekananda), in course of time, will acquire such powers for the benefit of the mankind. Thakur was convinced that Naren had that potential which required to be properly nurtured. Young men having such potential was indeed very rare in those days. On that realisation, with that end in view, he was grooming Naren's personality and *soul* for spiritual progress slowly and gradually.

As far as Naren was concerned, due to his spiritual practices, there had been some little progress in transmitting his spiritual powers to someone else by touch (that is, by sharing a slice of his *aura*). Although he could feel the presence of such powers, to a certain extent, in him – there was neither any opportunity nor any occasion to test whether it worked or not.

Suddenly, on an auspicious night, Naren felt a very strong urge to try it out. Thakur was upstairs and Naren and other disciples were downstairs. After all the puja rituals were over, Naren was alone with another close disciple of Thakur's – Kali Prasad Chandra (later Swami Abhedananda) in one corner of a room. Naren got immersed in deep meditation and asked Kali Prasad to touch Naren's right knee with his right hand. As soon as Kali Prasad did it, his right hand started shaking vigorously. After one or two minutes, Naren opened his eyes and asked him how he felt. Kali Prasad said that he felt as if he had an electric shock, as if someone had transmitted electricity in his body. When another person came and asked him how he had felt, he said: "I tried to keep my hand steady, but I just couldn't." Soon after, Kali Prasad got drowned in deep meditation – his whole body became stiff, his head and hands became bent as if he had a cerebral stroke. He was totally unconscious. All those present made Naren responsible for such a mess.

Paramhansa sent someone to bring Naren upstairs. When Naren came, Thakur said: "You have started expending your power when you have not earned enough – whatever you'd earned you have spent – there is no saving, no surplus. This way you'll get bankrupt. Only when you have high saving, you go for limited and measured expenditure. *(What possibly Thakur had meant that first you generate enough Violet aura at your Sahasrar Chakra level, then you start spending in small quantities. Now, you have more of Indigo than Violet aura – you had taken the wrong step.)*

Thakur said: "Don't get impatient – pursue your *sadhana* religiously; at the appropriate time, Mother Goddess will guide you how should you use your powers. Just see what have you done to Kali Prasad by transmitting your *bhava* on to him. He was pursuing a particular *bhava* in his own way, as it had suited him. You got it spoilt totally. It is like a foetus got aborted after six months of pregnancy. Whatever had to happen has happened, now never make such a mistake again. Anyway, the boy is lucky. His life has been saved. He could have died because of your wrong intervention."

Narendranath thought: "What a wonder! Thakur was upstairs and we were downstairs. He had come to know whatever had happened to us in great detail."

What was the outcome? Whatever progress Kali Prasad had made so far by following his own path and *bhava*, got totally spoilt and he became erratic and inconsistent in whatever he did. Although Ramakrishna tried his best to restore his normalcy, Kali Prasad did not become steady until long after Thakur passed away. (Reference 16)

'*Aura*' Sharing as a 'Kalpataru'

The date was 1st January, year 1886. For the last two weeks, Ramakrishna's devotees had brought the ailing *Avatar* to stay in a garden-house at Cossipore in far north of Calcutta. The renowned physician Dr. Mahendralal Sarkar had suggested that Thakur should be shifted from the congested locality of Calcutta to an open airy environment. Ever since he had come to reside at this place, Thakur had not descended from his room which was upstairs. Today, he was feeling a little better and wanted to go downstairs to take a walk in the garden, in the afternoon.

The clock had struck three. Thakur descended from upstairs with Latu (later Swami Adbhutananda), dressed in a red-bordered dhoti and a kurta. Because of the cold weather, he had covered himself up with a semi-woollen scarf having a red border. He had put on a cap to cover his head and both the ears. He had a pair of slippers to cover his bare feet. Latu took him outside in the garden across a big hall. Underneath a large mango tree in the garden, a few of Thakur's householder devotees were sitting and chatting. Finding Thakur approaching towards them, they were very happy. The famous playwright and director Girish Chandra Ghosh was amongst those present there. Girish was at the height of his devotion towards Thakur and he used to tell others about Ramakrishna's divine glory.

Ramakrishna walked towards the group underneath the tree and asked Girish: "What do you find in me that you have to share with others? Have you found anything special in me which you've not found in anyone else?" Girish poured out his true feelings about Thakur which immediately put Thakur in a *Bhav samadhi.* His face developed a radiant glow and in a half-awake mood, he said to everyone present: "Let good sense prevail on all of you". Those present immediately exclaimed: "Jai Ramakrishna", "Jai Ramakrishna" and they moved towards Thakur to get his blessings.

When the first man touched Thakur's feet, Thakur lifted him, made him stand, touched his chest and moved his hand upward and said: "Let good sense dawn on you!". He did it with the second man, and the third man, and so on. Only in the case of two persons, he said: "Your time has not come to take such blessings from me. You've to wait!".

Later, when the devotees whom he had touched and blessed were asked how they had felt, they unanimously said that they had felt as if they had some addictive substance but all of them agreed that they had experienced a supreme bliss. As a matter of fact, the *Avatar*, while touching the chest of a devotee had shared with him a thin slice of his *aura*. What would have happened, if he had shared a thick slice – a spiritual explosion perhaps, who knows?? (Reference 17)

The 'Income Centre' & 'Cost/Expenditure Centre' Concepts Related to *'Aura'* Sharing

These are some of my most favourite concepts that used to discuss in my workshops, which I'm now relating to *'Aura'* sharing.

Let us take the case of a family – a household. The earning members are 'Income Centres'. They are 'Cost/Expenditure Centres' too as expenses are incurred for meeting the costs of their food, clothes and other requirements. Those family members who are not earning, they are 'Cost/Expenditure Centres' but if they are really dedicated and wise, they would regard 'Cost/Expenditure Reduction & Control' as also their responsibility.

The same concept of mine I am now extending to '*Aura*'.

Sri Sri Ramakrishna used to spend from his '*aura*' by blessing whoever used to come to him by allowing that person to touch his feet and/or by he touching her/him on the head or embracing as he had embraced the temple sweeper Rasik who was mad to get his '*darshan*' and blessings. Interestingly, Ramakrishna's '*Aura*' 'Income Centre' was none else than Goddess Kali. *Avatars* can infuse life into a clay, stone, or metal image of a deity and talk to the God/Goddess, have sport (*Leela*) with Him/Her and, of course EARN energy ('*Aura*') from Him/Her.

A child who is reluctant to get down from the mother's lap, is STEALING '*Aura*' from the mother and if such practice continues with an ailing mother, it affects the mother's health and she becomes emaciated and anaemic if she belongs to a poor family and has a large number of kids.

Sri Sri Ramakrishna had a divine birth so although both her parents had crossed the middle age (father 60+ and mother 45+), he had no dearth of '*Aura*' ever. And, in Dakshineswar, he used to get a regular supply of '*Aura*' from the Goddess who was an eternal source of cosmic energy.

Young Narendra Nath had heard that '*sadhana*' gives one the power to transfer spirituality to another person by exercising willpower and also by touching her/him.

He used to do meditation and '*sadhana*' but had not attained a level when he could share a slice of his '*Aura*' with another person.

Without telling Ramakrishna anything, he experimented with the transfer of '*Aura*' to another disciple of Thakur and the consequence was disastrous. You might have already read about it in my last piece.

Aura and Consciousness

Avatar Ramakrishna had unending curiosity to know the unknowns. Once he had heard from some of his devotees that there is a scientific instrument available to see ordinarily invisible things very clearly and distinctly. Someone known to a devotee had only recently qualified as a medical doctor with flying colours and he had received a powerful microscope as a reward. He had brought his microscope to show Thakur what it can do, but Thakur said: "My mind is, at the moment, at such a high level of *consciousness* that I simply cannot bring it down to the level which will allow me to see through the instrument that you've so kindly brought." The devotees present waited for a long time to see if Thakur's consciousness could come down to a lower level, but it didn't even after a long waiting. So, the devotees used it to see microscopic organisms but as Thakur was not in a position to use it, the medical doctor took it back.

At the highest level of *aura* where the frequency of vibrations is very high, then one loses the physical (body) and other lower levels of consciousness (like hunger, thirst, sexual libido and so on). At that highly spiritual level, the Paramhansa used to have wonderful divine visions and his soul used to get totally detached from his body. He would not only lose his senses, but his heart beats will drop to the lowest level and his body will remain like that of a dead person. His thoughts will be totally free from anything related to the human existence – he will remain in the totally blissful state (*'satchidananda')*. Again when he descended from that higher level of *consciousness* with his *aura* colour changing and frequency of vibrations getting reduced, he would regain his 'body consciousness' and 'I' feeling like any normal person. He will again use his eyes to see things as we do, use his ears to hear as we do, use his taste buds to taste food and drinks as we do, he will use his nose to smell things as we do, and he would use his skin to have the touch feeling as we do, and use his mind to think and feel as we do.

This validates what the great Western philosopher Ralph Waldo Emerson had said: "Consciousness ever moves along a graded plane". (Reference 18) That was the perception of the ancient Indian sages also. Such graded *consciousness* was very much accessible to many *sadhak*s in ancient times. However, that powerhouse of the human brain had not been used for ages as, with the advent of science and technology, many of such powers that ancient age humans have been replaced with man-made systems, gadgets and accessories. Naturally, therefore, such super powers are accessible only to superhuman beings like highly evolved souls. Common people are anchored in the science & technology-centric civilised societies.

Avatar Ramakrishna never used to perceive things from only one angle as we do. He used to see things from a much higher plane how different people in the society think, how they behave, and how they act and react under different circumstances. That is why although he could his devotees and disciples thoroughly, it used to be difficult for them to understand him. They could not come up to his plane of perception and consciousness. Ordinary people see dogs, cows, foxes, hills, rivers and houses as they are perceived in the earthly, materialistic plane, he used to tell these objects were present in different containers like different pillows have different pillow cases or covers made of different styles and textures of textiles, but inside they all had cotton obtained from the same source – plants and trees that produce cotton. Similarly, different things – living as well as non-living have the same material inside – the unsliced *Soul – Satchidananda.* Thakur used to say as if Goddess Kali was peeping out from different outfits (the same image is dressed up in different dresses every day).

Thakur used to see the same Mother Goddess in every female – whether it was a child or an old woman, whether it was an unmarried virgin or a married housewife or an aged widow, whether it was a noble, decent lady or a prostitute.

When the *Avatar* used to be in the normal level of *consciousness*, he had much sharper and more alert senses and much superior intelligence than normal people, even though he was illiterate. (Reference 19)

Reflection of Your Emotions in the *Aura*

'Sada' Ripu's – 'Six Enemies of the Mind' get reflected in the *Aura.* Although we can't see it as the '*aura*' is invisible to the normal human eye, it gets reflected non-verbally through your body language, choice of words and tonal fluctuations. The only exception to such phenomenon are the *Avatars* like Sri Sri Ramakrishna.

There were occasions when Ramakrishna did not spare the use of Bengali slangs and abusive words but the negative effect used to be nullified by his high frequency 'God Consciousness' ('*Oishi Bhava*') '*aura*'. You and I being commonplace '*Veera*' or '*Naro*' *bhava* people won't be spared from the negative consequences of display of our negative emotions through negative words, negative body language and negative tone of voice. Others will be able to feel the negative vibrations and be repelled.

Your *aura* is your emotional emission – so you have to be watchful about your *aura* fluctuations and must make a point to do 'aura cleansing' regularly.

Sri Sri Ramakrishna used to avoid people who used to come for a meeting with some selfish motive like getting a favour such as curing a disease or winning in a court case. 'Opportunists' have their typical '*auras*'.

When the *Avatar* had high frequency vibrations with a very high quality '*aura*', others could feel from his beaming voice and a glow in his looks. And, during his such '*bhav*' or state of consciousness, whoever he touched, got his complete blessings. He used to say that he used to get a message regularly from Goddess Kali – 'Stay in a high level of consciousness' (In Bengali: '*Bhav mukhe thak*').

When two persons have '*auras*' vibrating at the same high frequency, the condition is what I would describe as '*Aura Resonance*'. This is what had made Ramakrishna and Sarada Devi a 'Divine Couple' – which is a very rare situation.

Normally, married couples suffer from a condition which I call '*Aura De-synchrony*' – the husband and the wife have their '*auras*' vibrating at different frequencies.

Even in a householder's life, the husband and the wife can achieve, at least once their kids have grown up into late teens, '*Aura Resonance*' if they both are devoted to the same God/Goddess with equal earnestness. That should be goal to achieve 'Happy Couplehood'.

'Biological *Aura*' versus 'Microbial *Aura*'

The '*aura*' that I have talked about so far is your 'Biological *Aura*'. How can we forget our 100 trillion microbes which are guests of the outside surface and inside cavities of our body?

Made up of millions, billions, trillions of bacteria, yeast, cells and cell parts, your 'Microbial Bubble', which looks like a cloud, is unique to you. It is your outer body's microbiome.

Your external cladding, the skin is like a vast savannah populated with millions of exotic critters. They feed on the oils seeping from your skin, dead cells, bits of organic matter and else. In a single centimetre of skin, you can find thousands of bacteria. (Reference 20)

Your microbiome cloud is what happens when your body liberates those gut and skin microbes. When you scratch your head or body surface, thousands of skin cells, cell fragments, bacteria and fungi get airborne. When you pick your nose or burp, microbes join the cloud.

If you are shaking hands with someone or hugging, you are placed in that person's microbial cloud. When someone walks by and you feel the breeze, you are allowing that person's microbes to enter into your field. The microbial clouds, just like the 'Biological *Aura*' clouds, vary significantly from person to person.

There was a time when Ramakrishna's desire to have a direct '*darshan*' ('live' experience) of Goddess Kali had turned into a severe anxiety. This mental state of his got manifested in his external physical symptoms. His chest would become blood-red, his eyes would become heavy and swollen with tears. He had lost his appetite and his sleep had reduced. Ever since he started his '*sadhana*', he had a burning sensation all over his body. It reached its peak in course of time. He suffered too much for six months.

When the burning situation was at its peak, he used to visualise a monster-like dark-skinned man in a drunken state who had entered into his body was walking in front of him. Then, suddenly once, he saw a noble monk came out of his body and killed the monster. From that moment, his burning sensation had completely disappeared. It was a boon from the Mother Goddess, it seemed which had resolved the conflict between Thakur's 'Biological *Aura*' and 'Microbial *Aura*'. (Reference 21)

References

[1] Dr. Brian Weiss, *Many Lives, Many Masters,* London: Piatkus, 1994.

[2] Dr. Brian Weiss, *Messages from the Masters*, London, Piatkus, 2000.

[3] Dr Brian Weiss, *Same Soul, Many Bodies*, London: Piatkus, 2004.

[4] "Aura" – *Wikipedia.*

[5] Jessica Estrada & Amelia McBride, "Each of the 7 Chakras Is Associated with a Color – Here's What Each One Means", *well + good,* Updated 7th November 2023.

[6] "A Guide to Chakra Colors and Their Spiritual Meanings", *Satya Jewelry,* 21st August, 2023.

[7] "Solfeggio Frequencies and Chakras", *Better Sleep,* 15th October, 2022.

[8] Dilip Kumar Ghosh, *Sri Sri Ramakrishna Punthi: Ek Akshay Shristi,* (In Bengali), Kolkata: Sahityasree, 2023, pp. 82–83.

[9] Sanjib Chattopadhyay, *Parama Pada Kamaley*, (Akhanda) (In Bengali), Kolkata: Udbodhan Karjalay, 2023, pp. 17–18.

[10] Dilip Kumar Ghosh, *Sri Sri Ramakrishna-Punthi: Ek Akshay Shristi* (In Bengali), Kolkata: Sahityasree, 2023, p. 8.

[11] "Whom Thakur Had Blessed by Placing His Feet on His Head?" (In Bengali) # shorts # youtubeshorts, Thakur Ma Swamiji Channel.

[12] "Whom Sarada Ma Had Blessed by Placing Her Feet on His Head?" (In Bengali), Video Presentation on YouTube; Thakur Ma Swamiji Channel.

[13] Sanjib Chattopadhyay, *Parama Pada Kamaley (Akhanda)* (In Bengali), Kolkata: Udbodhan Karjalaya, 2nd Edition, 31st Reprint, 2023, p. 503.

[14] "Three bodies doctrine" – *Wikipedia.*

[15] Dumuzzi, "Nirvikalpa Samadhi and what it is like to exist in a non-dual state", *reddit.com/r/hinduism*

[16] Swami Saradananda, *Sri Sri Ramakrishna Leela Prasanga: 1st Part: Sadhak Bhav,* (In Bengali) Kolkata: Udbodhan Karjalaya, 1993, pp. 3–6; Original Publication Year: 1914.

[17] Swami Saradananda, *Sri Sri Ramakrishna Leela Prasanga: 1st Part: Guru Bhav,* Kolkata: Udbodhan Karjalaya, 1993, pp. 59–62.

[18] "Ralph Waldo Emerson" – *Wikipedia.*

[19] Swami Saradananda, *Sri Sri Ramakrishna Leela Prasanga (2nd Part),* (In Bengali) Kolkata: Udbodhan Karjalaya, Bengali Year 1398, pp.148–150.

[20] Nick Stockton, "Your Body Is Surrounded by Clouds of Skin and Fart Bacteria", *WIRED*, 22nd September, 2015.

[21] Swami Saradananda, *Sri Sri Ramakrishna Leela Prasanga, Part 1, Sadhak Bhav,* Kolkata: Udbodhan Karjalaya, 1993, p. 65 & p. 73.

My Last Few Words

I have discussed a lot about the '*Poshu Bhava*' ('pre-human' nature), the '*Naro*' or the '*Veera Bhavas*' ('human nature') and the '*Divya Bhava*' ('post-human' nature) of the Hindu *Tantra*. '*Tamo*' guna' is predominant in the '*Poshu Bhava*') whereas in the latter two, the '*Rajo*' and '*Sattva*' gunas are more active respectively. (References 1 & 2)

If you conduct a systematic survey, you may find that although the '*Poshu Bhava*' may not be directly visible outside but it is very much dormant there, in the subconscious of those who are in the '*Naro/ Veera Bhava*' group. If you go a little deeper into the Hindu *Puranas*, you shouldn't be surprised to find that even gods and goddesses are not free from the *ripus (The Six Enemies of the Mind)* that keeps one way from the divine '*Divya Bhava*'. I am sharing one very interesting example with you.

Devi Ahalya was the wife of Maharishi Gautama. According to many Hindu *Puranas*, the King of the Gods, Devraj Indra allured her to share the same bed with him. (Certainly, it was a strong sign of '*Poshu Bhava*' – 'pre-human' state of mind). When Rishi Gautama came to know about such adulterous act of Indra, he threw a curse on him that his body would be filled with one thousand vulvas. That meant that Indra will have to cope with such massive menstruation from not just one or two but from one thousand vulvas every month and all the vulvas may not menstruate together (what a terrible bloody mess – indeed difficult to imagine). However, subsequently, some god or goddess or a sage might have had taken pity on Indra (he was the King of the Gods in Heaven, after all) and had reduced the punishment to one thousand eyes instead of vulvas. (References 3 & 4)

Some people have very strong '*Poshu Bhava*' due to the predominance of one or more of the *Sada Ripus ('Six Enemies of the Mind')*. If that happens, then the glow of his 'Biological *Aura*' will reduce leading to an increase in his 'Microbial *Aura*'. It happens when there is attraction for something grossly worldly.

Those, who have a very strong '*Naro Bhava*' ('human' propensities), they think more about themselves – they are 'SELF'-oriented. They are interested in 'TAKEs' – what they can GET from others to satisfy their own and their families' and friends' interests.

Those who are settled in '*Divya Bhava*' ('post-human' propensities), their attitude is just reverse. Under any circumstances, they think how they can repay the debts for what they have got from others – not only the principal but with interest also. They 'GIVE' selflessly, without expecting anything in return. They want to leave this planet 'EMPTY' without leaving any 'DEBT' with anyone. What kind of 'GIVEs' they concentrate on? They want to give to the society to which they belong – for its spiritual advancement. They want to contribute for the progress of their domain where they are operating. They want to GIVE to the whole world. They feel this 'GIVE' is going to GOD.

They genuinely feel that they are getting everything from GOD (may be *via* someone or some organisation) and thus they are liable to return the principal with interest in this lifetime.

So, what is our finding? One who is in '*Divya Bhava*', he is MAD about GIVING to GOD for whatever he has already got from him. He is not MAD about GETTING anything worldly. He is not hungry for the pleasure chemical 'Dopamine' ('D'). Those who are in '*Poshu*' and '*Naro/Veera Bhavas*', they have unsatiated 'Dopamine Hunger' all the time.

Having spent so much time with the *Avatar* Sri Sri Ramakrishna, this is my conclusion. These are my last few words. The *Avatar* was never MAD. *Avatars* are misunderstood by common people. And, Sri Sri Ramakrishna was no exception. Those who took him as a mad man, were MAD themselves!!

References

[1] "The Three Temperaments" – *TantraMag*, 6th January 2016.

[2] "Complete Guide to the 3 Gunas of Nature: Sattva, Rajas & Tamas", *Arhanta Yoga*, 2nd August 2019.

[3] "Ahalya: The Woman Who Was Cursed into a Stone", *RTISTIQ*.

[4] "How is Indra punished for seducing Ahalya?" *Quora*.

[5] Pallavi Thakur, "The real story of Ahalya: When Lord Indra was cursed for lust!" *Speakingtree.in* 22nd July, 2015.